Struggle and Suffrage
in
Nottingham

Struggle and Suffrage in Nottingham

Women's Lives and the Fight for Equality

Carol Lovejoy Edwards

PEN & SWORD
HISTORY

AN IMPRINT OF PEN & SWORD BOOKS LTD
YORKSHIRE - PHILADELPHIA

First published in Great Britain in 2019 by
Pen & Sword History
An imprint of
Pen & Sword Books Ltd
Yorkshire – Philadelphia

ISBN 978 1 52671 210 3

Printed and bound in England
by TJ International, Padstow, Cornwall
Typeset in 11.5/14 point Times New Roman
by Aura Technology and Software Services, India

Pen & Sword Books Limited incorporates the imprints of Atlas,
Archaeology, Aviation, Discovery, Family History, Fiction, History,
Maritime, Military, Military Classics, Politics, Select, Transport, True
Crime, Air World, Frontline Publishing, Leo Cooper, Remember When,
Seaforth Publishing, The Praetorian Press, Wharncliffe Local History,
Wharncliffe Transport, Wharncliffe True Crime and White Owl.

For a complete list of Pen & Sword titles please contact
PEN & SWORD BOOKS LIMITED
47 Church Street, Barnsley, South Yorkshire, S70 2AS, England
E-mail: enquiries@pen-and-sword.co.uk
Website: www.pen-and-sword.co.uk

Or

PEN AND SWORD BOOKS
1950 Lawrence Rd, Havertown, PA 19083, USA
E-mail: Uspen-and-sword@casematepublishers.com
Website: www.penandswordbooks.com

Contents

Foreword

In researching this book, I have come across many fantastic women from Nottingham. One or two of them you will have heard of, like Helen Watts the Suffragette. Many you will not have heard of. Even so, their contribution to women's rights and freedoms has been immeasurable. Most of these women worked tirelessly to aid other less fortunate women wherever they could. They did not shout about it or seek praise and thanks. They just did it. I am proud to be a Nottingham woman I am thankful for the women who came before, making it much easier for me to undertake my chosen career path.

When researching this period of time, I came across the account of Angela Lesley Bates who recited a poem written in her autograph book by her mother in the 1930s. It read:

'Be a good girl, lead a good life.

Find a good husband, be a good wife.'

Times have changed and no longer is finding a good husband a woman's only ambition.

Introduction

Women's lives changed immensely during the hundred years between 1850 and 1950. Their place in the world had altered and so too had the freedoms they were allowed. Our lives today would be unrecognisable to a woman from the 1850s.

Although some areas of a woman's life had changed in the century to 1950, even by then, much remained the same in certain ways. We were still under the control of our fathers or our husbands, not allowed to have a bank account in our own name without our husbands' permission, and certainly not entitled to equal pay or even equal opportunity.

The woman who married, even if for economic reasons, became the property of her husband together with all her assets. My research revealed that a widow or a spinster often chose to stay single for reasons of independence, both economic and emotional.

Census records are a valuable research tool that enlighten us as to the occupations of our ancestors and the size of their families. Although information in the census can tell us what women were employed in doing, and how many children they had, it doesn't tell us how much they earned or what they wanted from life.

What the census cannot tell us are the conditions our ancestors lived in. There is no mention of how many houses were crammed into a small area, called a Yard, or how they shared a water pump and a privy; how that privy was emptied at night and the way that it spread disease among the occupants of many of these Yards. The census makes no mention of the heartbreak of infant mortality nor of the long hours worked in servitude to a master, whether in the factory, at the pit or in domestic service.

In 1851, 270,427 people were packed into an area of 526,076 acres in Nottinghamshire. Of those, 132,263 were men and 138,164 women.

By 1951, the figures had risen to 411,257 men and 429,954 women, making a total of 841,211; 6,594 households in 1951 had no piped water and 89,781 had no fixed bath. Astonishingly, the number of households without a WC in 1951 was 15,682.

We consider these to be essentials today. However, for previous generations, indoor plumbing must have seemed quite a luxury.

Data from 1881 reveals that eight per cent of Nottinghamshire's female population worked in service. There were five times as many women as men working as domestic servants.

Women's lives have improved in great leaps over the century 1850–1950. But these changes did not come easily. There were bloody battles along the way, costing many women a great deal. These women had numerous hardships to endure, including four major wars: Crimean, Boer, First and Second World War; women followed their men to the Crimean peninsula, South Africa and in the latter two wars, became nurses, tram drivers and munitions workers. There was poverty and malnutrition as well as disease, and the exhaustion of working and raising a family while being treated less favourably than men in all areas of their lives.

Gradually, women have entered all aspects of previously male dominated life and proved themselves to be equal to – while being different from – men.

CHAPTER ONE

The Struggle for Knowledge

Timeline of Statutes

1870 Forster Elementary Education Act: Board schools managed by elected school boards, were set up, and partially funded by the state, to provide elementary education in areas where existing provision was deemed inadequate.

1880 Elementary Education Act: made education compulsory up to the age of 10.

1891 Elementary Education Act: made provision for education to be paid for by the government.

1893 Elementary Education (School Attendance) Act: raised the school leaving age to 11 and then later to 13.

1897 Voluntary Schools Act: gave grants to public elementary schools not funded by school boards.

1900 Higher Elementary Schools: schools were recognised and provided education for children aged 10 to 15.

1902 Balfour's Education Act: created Local Education Authorities which took responsibility for Board Schools.

1918 Fisher Education Act: made secondary education compulsory up to the age of 14. Also made the state responsible for secondary education schools.

1919 Sex Disqualification (Removal) Act: allowed women to work in the law and in the civil service. 'A person shall not be disqualified by sex or marriage from the exercise of any public function or from being appointed to or holding any civil or judicial office or post, or from (Section 1) entering or assuming or carrying on any civil profession or vocation or for admission to any incorporated society.'

1929 Local Government Act: brought Poor Law schools into state funding.

1936 Education Act: proposed raising the school leaving age to 15. It was postponed due to the war.

1944 Butler Education Act: split education into primary and secondary with the age of 11 being the age for moving from one to the other. The marriage bar for teachers was abolished by this act.

1947: the school leaving age was raised to 15.

1951: 'O' and 'A' levels introduced.

Even with all the improvements made by 1950, education for women was based largely around the idea of training women to be mothers and wives. In the years since 1950, women have been given opportunities to become scientists, engineers and even astronauts.

School Life and Teaching

The 1870 Education Act authorised the setting up of School Boards in any area where existing voluntary provision was inadequate. The Acts of 1876 and 1880 brought compulsory education for children up to the age of 10. Girls and boys did the three 'R's – Reading Writing and Arithmetic, but the girls then had extra lessons in domestic subjects, such as needlework, preparing them for domestic service or for their forthcoming lives as wives and mothers.

After the 1902 Act, education became the responsibility of the counties and country boroughs. Headmasters were obliged to keep records of events and activities in school and the log book often showed regular absences when children were helping in the home by caring for relatives; helping parents out with their lace 'out work', or working in the fields alongside their parents at harvest time. Lowdham National School records show that, on 13 July 1863, thirty-two girls were absent. Eight were nursing relatives;

five were haymaking; four were singling turnips (thinning out the plants so the remainder can thrive); three were washing; three had no money; two had bad feet; two had a bad hand and one was doing general work.

Early in the twentieth century the traditional emphasis on domestic education for girls, including needlework, cookery and laundry, was widened to cover all domestic training. Part of the reason for this was the desire to combat disease and poverty by raising standards of hygiene and health in the home through education. The education authority in Nottingham established a ladies' subcommittee to advise the Elementary and Secondary School subcommittee on all matters of domestic training for school girls. The subcommittee dealt with the adaptation of premises for domestic training; arranged for the supply of domestic materials, for needlework and cookery; advised on staffing matters and also on medical developments that the schools needed to teach to the girls.

The girls could go on a six-week training course, at one of two homes in Nottingham, to learn all aspects of the work involved in running a small household. One of these homes, Raleigh Street House, was equipped as an ordinary house, while the other at Forest Fields Centre, was set up as a small flat.

Mothercraft courses were also developed, with regular liaison between committee members, headmistresses and the medical profession. By the 1920s mothercraft lessons had become widely taught in Nottingham's schools. These lessons included practical tuition in bathing a baby (a washable doll), caring for the baby and putting it to bed in a cot made by the boys of the school.

The subcommittee also oversaw the provision of school meals, suggesting improvements where necessary.

Teaching was one of the few professions open to women before the twentieth century. Salaries were poor, less than the male teachers; hours were long and only single women were allowed to hold teaching posts, until as late as 1944. Married women were presumed to devote themselves to their husbands and children at home.

Most teachers entered the profession by the pupil teacher system introduced in 1846. Children as young as 13 would be given a five-year apprenticeship and be allowed to go to teacher training colleges. Once they had passed the college examinations they would achieve Certified Teacher status. Less able students could become uncertified teachers or assistant teachers. Most women earned only sixty-five per cent of the men's wage. Although women were allowed to be teachers (including married women from 1944), most women gradually began to enter other professions, yet the number of women qualifying as professionals remained low and it was still unusual to see women practise as doctors or lawyers.

In February 1928, the women's section of the *The Nottingham Journal* posed the question 'should the sexes be apart in schools?' This had been discussed by Dr F. Granger, Vice Principal of University College Nottingham and the ladies from the National Council of Women, Nottingham and Notts Branch. Dr Granger said that the advantages of mixing the sexes were threefold. Firstly, they met on equal terms on neutral ground; secondly, when men and women went out into the world they were able to mix more easily, and thirdly, they were able to assess each other as possible partners. Even the enlightened men of the era, who believed in education for women, still could not release the idea that women should fulfil their traditional roles at the same time. Progress may have been slow, but it was progress nonetheless.

However, Granger did not agree with mixing the sexes before the age of 18 saying that those between and 14 and 18 years old, when the girl is a 'hoyden' and the lad is a 'hobbledehoy', should definitely be kept apart.

Mr B.W.L. Bulkeley, Director of Education for Nottinghamshire, commented that the Education Committee were against all mixed education if they could avoid it, except for children under 11. The reasons he gave were that it would lead to 'retardation' and strain on the boys. He went on to say that he thought girls needed restraining from their books.

Both Bulkeley and Granger agreed that separating the sexes at 11 would give the girls a better chance. It was also noted that once a boy had finished his school day his time was his own, whereas a girl then had to help with childcare and housework, perpetuating traditional roles while recognising that girls needed better opportunities.

The debate was still raging some two years later when it was discussed by Nottingham University College on 14 October 1930. The *Nottingham Evening Post* on 26 November 1926 carried an article claiming that Nottingham schools were out of date, following a government official's report.

W.E. Morris, BSc., stated that 'freer mixing would lead to a truer understanding of womankind and the psychological tendency to self-display might be harnessed for educational advantage.'

Mr A.F. Orton disagreed. He argued that education was to make a man fit to live and fit to live with. If women were being educated alongside men, they would be seeing the unfinished article. Miss Marjorie Wright, in favour of coeducation, claimed that it would make men more refined and women much more sensible. She said that, 'the boarding-school girl who had been brought up to look upon a man as a forbidden, and therefore particularly interesting species, either became very shy, or, an individual eternally wrangling about women's rights.'

However, not all women were in favour of women being educated. Miss Ella Saunders BA said that since the war the rise of coeducation had created 'sexless creatures with a superficial veneer of courtesy and similar interests'. Thankfully, these women were in the minority.

Mr J.L. Payne declared that this was the most immoral age ever seen. The vote returned was 29:19 in favour of single-sex education. It was clear that some men struggled with the notion of education, let alone equality, for women.

Nottingham High School for Girls celebrated its 75th Anniversary in September 1950 with a thanksgiving service in St Mary's Church in the Lace Market. The founders, Canon Francis Morse, vicar of St Mary's and Dr John Brown Paton, Principal of Paton College, were remembered in prayers. Among those in the congregation were the Vice Chancellor of Nottingham University, B.L. Hallward, and the Director of Education for Nottingham, Mrs Hallward. The Bishop of Southwell, Mr F.R. Barry, said: 'As from one generation to another, more and more women move out from it (the High School) and into the world. Its influence extends in widening circles into the outlook of our whole community and it is a force that is powerful for good.' The bishop went on to say that these schools had done more than their founders could have foreseen to enrich the whole quality of national life by lifting the quality of women's education. Many women from the High School went onto university and the school had set the standard for the rest of the country. 'No movement had done more to overcome the prejudices, the inertia and the false values', which had been in the path of women seeking education. He also stated that we needed education to provide the free-thinking, independent minds upon which our democracy depended.

Professionals

According to the *Nottingham Evening Post*, on 5 March 1918, shortly after women over 30 became enfranchised, the second Bill allowing women to become solicitors passed through the House of Lords without objection or discussion. It then became The Sex Disqualification (Removal) Act 1919. Its purpose was to amend the Law with respect to disqualification by reason of sex or marriage. The first women solicitors were admitted in 1922, when four women passed the Law Society's exams.

A participant in an oral history project in Nottingham in the 1980s (the participants were largely kept anonymous), spoke of when she qualified as a doctor in 1925. She had attended the Girls' High School in Nottingham followed by university in London. She worked as a locum for quite some time when she first qualified as permanent jobs were hard to come by.

When the doctor set up her own practice around 1926, she did so in a brand-new bungalow at 39 Middleton Boulevard. The hall was the waiting room and the second reception room was the surgery. This doctor also helped at the City Hospital in the isolation ward and also in the Smallpox Hospital in Bulwell.

The doctor used a Morris Minor to get to and from home and around to her patients. She later became a District Medical Officer, while still running her Wollaton Park practice under the Poor Laws, which meant that she spent most of her time in and out of peoples' homes. She covered the Meadows, including Arkwright Street, and all the way down to Lenton Abbey.

Immediately before the National Health Service came into being she had 2,500 patients. Quite a few of these were wealthy patients who paid her in cash. She also had what were known as 'panel patients'. These patients paid weekly amounts into a scheme to ensure their medical bills would be covered when help was needed. During the Second World War one of her male colleagues had joined up and she oversaw his practice as well as her own, giving a certain percentage of her fees to him.

Post School Years

At a meeting of the National Council for Women in November 1933, A.H. Whipple, Director of Education for Nottingham, said the education committee was working side by side with the voluntary institutions. The city now maintained six institutes for women with a total membership of 2,600.

A 1937 Exhibition at the Nottingham Albert Hall showcased the talents of all ages from the Clarendon Institute for Women, which provided classes for women in a variety of subjects. Among the exhibits were contributions from four generations of one family. The family was not named but their exhibits were musical appreciation (great-grandmother) upholstery (grandmother) domestic science (mother) and commercial subjects (daughter). Miss D. Moore, principal of the Institute, called for a technical college for women in Nottingham, stating that the already large number of enrolees at the Institute, some 1,300 aged between 14 and 70, proved the need for such a college. The classes available at the Institute were still predominantly in women's subjects of the time: cookery, keep fit, sewing and first aid among others.

Lady Atkey who opened the event said that one of the country's greatest needs was to educate women – so that they would make good and careful wives and look after their husbands well. While great strides were being made in affording women more opportunities it would take much longer for attitudes, including those of women themselves, to be changed.

On 9 July 1928, *The Nottingham Journal* proudly declared that the path to knowledge and culture was now open to all. It displayed pictures of several of the women staff members at the university college, including Miss Bramfield, MA History; Miss Chesters, BSc Zoology; Miss E.R. Collie, MA PhD Psychology; Mrs Kirkaldy, Music; Miss Browning, PhD Physics; Miss Bexon, MSc Botany and Miss H.J. Hutchinson, Physiology and Warden of Foreign Students.

Lady Boot, wife of the founder of the university college, Lord Jesse Boot, donated funds for the women's hostel at the university. The author of the article, one Helen Wright, commented how the early women pioneers in education had suffered prejudice and ridicule but had continued with their quest and now women of the time could enjoy an education without suffering such contempt and derision. It was thought that, with these strong women coming before them, local women would have everything in the hoped-for university, to encourage them to succeed. The articles ends, 'May the future University of Nottingham be the 'alma mater' of many a woman whose name will go down to posterity along with those pioneers whose footsteps she will have so honourably followed.'

Some years before the comments of J.L. Payne, in September 1895 (see above), *The Nottingham Evening Post* praised Nottingham Technical School for Women, which would lead you to believe that science or engineering would be on the curriculum. However, this was a training school for teachers, formed by the Nottingham and District School for Cookery and the Nottingham Ladies' Sanitary Association, with premises at 63 Long Row in the heart of the city, which was empowered to grant diplomas in cookery and laundry work. There were nine teachers of cookery, eight for laundry work, two for domestic economy, five on dressmaking, one on millinery and fourteen on sanitation and sick nursing. In addition, more than twenty girls were taking their teaching diplomas in the subjects. Dr Boobbyer, Medical Health Officer for the city, was one of the committee members overseeing the work of the school.

At a meeting with the National Council for Women, Nottingham and Notts Branch, on 11 December 1933, education director for the city, A.H. Whipple, praised the voluntary organisations who worked alongside the Education Committee in Nottingham. The city maintained six education centres providing evening classes to some 2,600 women.

A meeting of the Notts. Federation of Women's Institutes held at the Mikado Café on 20 April 1937 brought education to the fore of the discussion again. Miss Grace Hadow, warden of the Society of Oxford Home Students, was the speaker at the event and declared that the mind needed as much exercise as the body, and should not be allowed to become 'bedridden'. Education was a tool to provide the wisdom to stay away from evil and embrace the good in life, she claimed, adding that the purpose of education was to make life richer and happier.

B.D.W. Blakeley also attended the meeting and talked about the reorganisation going on in the city schools. Classes were being segregated into different age groups and then again by subject so that specialist teaching could be provided. He said that new schools would have to be built to accommodate these arrangements. This was essentially the start of the education system as we would recognise it today.

The Nottingham Co-operative Society and its educational activities were the subject of a report in the *Journal* on 6 November 1929. From seven meetings in 1922–23 the society now held forty-four meetings in the year 1927–28. During that year 17,000 people attended the gatherings, an average of 400 per gathering. Classes included bookkeeping, salesmanship, and ticket writing while several important speakers and lecturers had visited Nottingham including MPs and one Lord to the Admiralty.

While formal education was limited for young girls and women, the many social and charitable organisations ensured that opportunities for women were available as often as possible.

CHAPTER TWO

The Working Life

❖

Timeline of Statutes

1870 Factories Act: the total hours which could be worked by a woman were limited to sixty per week.

1867 Factories (Extension) Act: women and children could no longer work on Sundays.

1871 Bank Holidays Act: made official holidays of Easter Monday, Whit Monday (in May) and 26 December.

1872 Metalliferous Mines Regulation Act: no women or girls were allowed in mines.

1874 Factories Act: the working day was limited to ten hours for women between 6 a.m. and 6 p.m. The working week was limited to 56½ hours.

1891 Factory and Workshop Act: no factory owner could employ a woman within four weeks of her giving birth.

1917 Women's Land Army established.

1917 Women's Royal Naval Reserve.

1918 Women's Royal Air Force established.

1938 Women's Royal Voluntary Service for Civil Defence.

1939 Women's Land Army re-launched.

1941 National Service Act: introduced conscription for women. All unmarried women between the ages of 20 and 30 were called up for war work. It was later extended to include women up to the age of 43 and to include married women. Those women who were pregnant or had young children could be exempted.

1941 Trades Union Congress: supported the principle of equal pay (which finally arrived in 1975).

1946 Royal Commission on Equal Pay: recommends that teachers, local government officers, civil servants should all receive equal pay.

1946 Marriage Bar: was abolished in the Post Office, civil service and the BBC.

The Nottingham Daily Express on 12 January 1886, printed a letter in the 'Women's Work' section about the second Exhibition of Women's Industries. It stated,

> It is most remarkable that we have had to wait until now for a fair exposition of the share women take in the business of production. Their place in the counting house at the desk and in our public offices has only just been granted to them. There are some indications of women being permitted, in a very harmless degree, to make money by trade. All the wit, so far, was men's. All the learning all of art, they held without check or competition and nearly all the business too.

The letter writer signed herself 'The Queen'.

When women went out to work it was often an extension of their duties at home, with domestic service being a common, low-paid, occupation. Other women worked in the many lace and textile factories in Nottingham. This would also be low-paid work and opportunities were strictly limited.

During two world wars women showed that they were capable of much more, although it was not until after this period that the greatest changes were made, for instance the Equal Pay Act of 1970, which came into force in 1975, made it unlawful to pay a woman less for the same job carried out by a man.

Pre-1914

The 1851 Census records show that the majority of women in the Nottingham area were occupied as housewives, the next largest category being domestic servants or housekeepers. The remainder were mostly lace workers or dressmakers.[1] Traditional roles in and around the home were the majority of opportunities available to women.

The growth of the lace industry brought more opportunities for women to earn a living, usually from home as 'out workers'. In the prosperous pre-First World War years, Thomas Adams employed nearly 1,400 people, the majority of them women, at its Stoney Street premises.[2] These women were engaged in lace dressing, scalloping, knitting, bleaching and making up of ladies' wear.

The employment of women in cycle and other manufacturing workshops (Nottingham had the leading light in Raleigh Cycles) became widespread with the introduction of mass-production techniques in the early 1900s. Even so, women were limited in what kind of jobs within these industries they were allowed to tackle. A letter in the *Scottish Cycles* magazine drew attention[3] to Raleigh where women were employed 'only upon work which suits their physique and temperament and upon which they are more skilful and quicker than men'.

Raleigh, like other large Nottingham firms of the time, appointed a welfare supervisor. Lily Barter worked for Raleigh from the First World War until her retirement in 1937, ensuring that the women had adequate working conditions and helping with their family and personal problems when required.

Mrs Ball [4], born in 1895, worked as an errand girl for Kerry and Carriers in Byard Lane when she left school in 1909. She told how she had to go out on a bicycle with a wicker basket and take lace parcels to the different factories. Two of them worked together and they would take it in turn riding in the basket on the way back to the factory once all the deliveries had been made. She worked there until she was 15, receiving four shillings a week, until her mother became ill and she had to stay at home to look after her. Many young women had to give up their jobs to stay at home and look after ailing or elderly relatives, young children or to keep house for their widowed fathers.

After her mother died in 1910, Mrs Ball's father took her to Boots on Island Street where she was taken on and earned around five shillings per week. At that time, Boots was a well-known Nottingham company, established in 1849 as a herbal medicine shop by John Boot, and employed a large number of local people.

Her job involved labelling bottles of medicines and hair cream and packing them in boxes of dozens or half dozens. The boxes then went along the conveyor belt where they were sealed up by someone else. She recalled seeing Jesse Boot (John's son and then owner of the company) on one occasion when he visited the Island Street factory; she described him as 'looking quite frail'.

Although Mrs Ball doesn't specify a date, she did confirm that upon her marriage to a fellow employee she had to leave Boots; she also stated that she never knew how much her husband earned. Mrs Ball also recalled how, during the Second World War her husband would refuse to go into the air raid shelters and many times the warden would bang on their door, urging them to go.

Prior to 1914, many women carried out domestic work for others to try to make ends meet. Sometimes their own children had to be taken along, either because of childcare issues or to help earn money.

Mrs Robinson,[5] born on Denman Street in Radford to a family who were show people, had twenty siblings and then ten of her own children, six of whom survived into adulthood. She recalls the living conditions when she had her first house, as a married woman, in 1913 in Carrington, about how they had to go down the 'entry, round the back,' for the water, and the lavatory was round the back too. When the children came she tells how she went out 'scrubbin' and cleanin' tekkin the kids wi' me too.' For this work, she earned 1s 6d a day.

When her husband became ill with tuberculosis and could no longer work, she had to feed and clothe the whole family. She used the pawn shop often, taking flat irons, her corsets or anything else that was not absolutely necessary. She lived in a back-to-back house with concrete floors and no carpets, and meals were cooked on the open fire.

The Great War

During the First World War, known at the time as the Great War, women took over the jobs left open by men joining up. They became window cleaners, tram conductors, post deliverers and munitions workers, as well as continuing to work in factories that had now turned their attention to the war effort.

During the war, a huge effort was made by the women of Nottingham to meet the needs of war work. The committee responded to a letter from the Portsmouth Branch of the National Union of Women Workers (NUWW) asking for particulars of the conditions under which women tram conductors were working in Nottingham. Most of those employed in the city had family members serving in one branch or another of the armed forces. Unusually, for these times, the women were paid the same as the men. The committee also heard reports of the women window cleaners at work in Nottingham. The girls started on eighteen shillings per week and worked from 7 a.m. to 5 p.m.

The industrial committee of the Nottingham NUWW had welcomed three groups of girls (reported in July 1916) coming to work in munitions in Nottingham. They had been escorted to the Labour Exchange and then helped to find suitable lodgings. In December 1916, the committee were asked to provide information to the national committee on how many women were working on the land in Nottinghamshire. In January 1917 a tabulated report was read out to the committee from the information gleaned but unfortunately, the information was not recorded in the minutes.

Many local girls took the chance to work in the well-paid munitions factories in Nottingham, two of which were built in 1915 due to a national shell shortage; one at King's Meadow and the other at Chilwell. Lottie Martin, a participant in an oral history project in the early 1980s, told of her experiences at the Chilwell factory; she had worked the overhead crane which moved the shells from one part of the factory to another. The crane was accessed by a rope ladder, which Lottie hated as it would swing from side to side when she climbed it. She told the oral history project that she would only go to the toilet at lunchtimes or after her shift, to save having to go up and down that ladder again.

These girls were known as Canary Girls, as the chemical in the explosives turned their skin yellow. On 1 July 1918, there was an explosion in the Chilwell depot, killing 134 people, only 32 of whom could be positively identified. The explosion caused the largest loss of life during a single explosion during the Great War. The unidentified bodies are buried together in a mass grave at St Mary's Church, Attenborough.

Winston Churchill, Minister of Munitions at the time, sent a telegraph offering his condolences. It said:

> Please accept my sincere sympathy with you all in the misfortune that has overtaken your fine Factory and in the loss of valuable lives, those who have perished have died at their stations on the field of duty and those who have lost their dear ones should fortify themselves with this thought, the courage and spirit shown by all concerned both men and women command our admiration, and the decision to which you have all come to carry on without a break is worthy of the spirit which animates our soldiers in the field. I trust the injured are receiving every care.

A telegram was also sent from Buckingham Palace on behalf of the King. Lottie Martin described the day:

> The accident happened about five minutes to seven. I was at the kitchen sink when the terrible explosion happened. The day had been very hot, and the window was wide open, the vibration blew it in and everything, including the house, moved. I looked up to the window and a huge mushroom spiral of smoke and debris was rising in the sky.
>
> We made our way to the High Road but what a scene of horror met us. Every available vehicle had been commandeered to take

casualties to the hospitals. Men, women and young people, burnt practically all their clothing, bleeding with limbs torn off and eyes and hair literally gone.

We came back home after midnight but still the conveyances were making their way to Nottingham. The High Road, Beeston, had never before seen a cavalcade such as this. I believe there were about 120 mutilated corpses laid in the church at Attenborough, most of them unrecognisable. Others, who were not so bad and who were identified by their relatives, were buried privately.

The following Monday, along with other women and men, we represented the shift of the filling store. Every workplace had their own mourners. This awesome cavalcade wended its way down Attenborough Lane to the strains of the works band, playing the Death March.

It has never been fully established what caused the explosion.

In *The Times* on 9 July 1918, Mr F.G. Kellaway, MP and Parliamentary Secretary to Winston Churchill, speculated that the factory should be awarded the Victoria Cross. While this did not come to fruition, it is clear, that the men and women who perished on 1 July 1918 gave their lives for the war effort and should be remembered as having done so.

The Great War was the first war to affect almost everyone and the first war to actually be brought to our domestic doorstep. The Zeppelin raids in September 1916 caused three deaths and an enormous amount of damage as the bombs dropped on the city centre and Arkwright Street area. This tragedy superseded anything seen to date by the people of Nottingham.

Women also turned their hand to farm work, with the formation of the Women's Land Army in 1917. Thousands upon thousands of women were recruited, with the average wage being around thirty-two shillings per week. Uniforms were free with earth-coloured breeches; a green jersey; dungarees for working in and an overcoat for the winter. The Nottingham Land Army county office was at The Kennels, Thoresby Park, Ollerton. The service was disbanded on 30 November 1919.

Second World War

The Women's Land Army was resurrected in June of 1939 in preparation for the likely outbreak of war, with Lady Denman at its helm once more.

Although agriculture was a reserved occupation, many farmworkers had joined up. If land girls had not filled the gaps, as they had in the Great War, the German U-boat blockades may have worked and there would not have been enough food to go around our besieged country.

During the Second World War, arable land increased in area by sixty-three per cent, wheat, barley and potato crops almost doubled, and production rose by two-thirds. The number of tractors between 1942 and 1944 increased by fifty per cent and the total number of agricultural workers increased by twenty-two per cent.

One of the slogans that tempted women into the Land Army was 'For a Healthy, Happy Job, join the Women's Land Army.' Many, many women did so, and discovered just how much hard work there was in tending the land. By 1944[6] there were 67,000 Land Girls across the country, with a further 13,000 in the Women's Timber Corps (WTC), nicknamed the 'Lumber Jills', set up in 1942. The WTC were responsible for felling trees to provide pit props for the mines. Without them there would have been a severe coal shortage as homes, industry and transport heavily relied on coal supplies.

Many farms in Nottinghamshire took on land girls and, where accommodation was not available on the farm, hostels were established, for example in Woodhill School at Collingham and in the village hall in Hockerton.

Muriel Ward (née Wild) of Wollaton, Nottingham, recounted her life in the Timber Corps in the *Nottingham Evening Post*, 20 March 1995. She described the WTC as being one of the best-kept secrets of the war. Home-grown timber was essential during the war and with many men fighting overseas, it was up to the women to step into the forests to take over the measuring, felling, haulage, and sawmilling work which had traditionally been the domain of men. Muriel joined the WTC aged 20 and told how they only had two travel passes a year because they were classed as civilians. As Muriel had worked for the Civil Service in Nottingham, a reserved occupation, she had to apply for permission to join the Land Army, which was given in 1942. Muriel trained in sawmilling and loved it. The training was held at a camp in Bury St Edmunds and Muriel recalled how they still had time to relax. At one dance, the Highland Light Infantry were present in their kilts. The land girls were the only ones wearing trousers that night!

Muriel recalls that the manager of the first sawmill she was posted to greeted her by saying he didn't want women, but supposed he was 'stuck with them'. Muriel worked on a bench cutting the tree trunks down to various sizes. She was also the first aider and the firefighter. Her second posting, in 1944, was to Brown's Timber in Wollaton where she worked on a planer, cutting smaller pieces of wood to size for making utility furniture, horses' shafts (attached to the cart and then to the horses' tack) and even hockey sticks. Muriel told how her work mates were mostly men and included German prisoners of war who were camped at Wollaton Park.

In the evenings Muriel had to walk the prisoners back to their camp and remembers she never once felt afraid being in charge of the prisoners.

Joan Sewell was so enamoured of the farming life when she joined the WLA that she married the farmer's son! When she was 22, in 1941, Joan became a land girl and was sent to a hostel in Bunny, where she lived with thirty-one other girls. These girls were sent to various farms in the area to help with sugar beet, milking, and general chores. Joan particularly remembers the team spirit. She described the uniform as being a khaki shirt, green pullover and breeches which laced down the side. They would wear either boots or wellingtons and for really dirty work wore dungarees.

She married the farmer's son on 5 May 1945, wearing a turquoise dress with a gold studded collar, navy blue hat, shoes and gloves, which she had saved her clothing coupons to buy. The beginning of her married life was the ending of the war and start of peace time.

One of the overriding images when reading the land girls' stories were the special friendships that were formed between the women, some of them lasting a lifetime.

In 2008, Gordon Brown awarded a small certificate and a badge to all the women who had served in the Land Army, with a right to representation at the Remembrance Day service held at the Cenotaph, Whitehall, every year. Hilary Benn, the Environment Secretary at the time, said,

> it is absolutely right that we at last recognise the selfless efforts these women made to support the nation through the dark days of World War One and World War Two. This badge is a fitting way to pay tribute to their determination, courage and spirit in the face of adversity. I hope that as many eligible women as possible will apply for one.

It is unclear why these women could not be awarded the badge without having to make an application. Gordon Brown admitted that 'We have been slow to thank you. We could have done this years ago but I'm pleased that we can do it now. We owe you a huge debt of gratitude.' It is a shame that their recognition was so late in coming, too late for some of the women, who had already passed away.

The Women's Land Army was finally disbanded in 1950, some five years after the end of the war.

During the war, the Electrical Association for Women (EAW) helped out with the Women's Voluntary Service knitting and hospital supply schemes as well as mobile canteens. The national executive of the EAW took part in the discussion about post-war reconstruction at the fourth annual meeting on 24 February 1943. The President, Mrs A.B. Lewis, was in the chair and praised the work being done on the programme. She said that women needed to enter more into public life and should insist on having their opinions heard.

The Nottingham Journal on 27 November 1941 reported that a parade would be held the following Sunday, 30 November, in Nottingham of approximately 1,500 women war-workers. This was the idea of the Lord Mayor of Nottingham (Councillor L. Pillsworth) and was thought to be the first of the kind in the country to celebrate the contribution of women, both in uniform and in industry, to the war effort. The parade was to include members of the women's uniformed services, together with secretaries from the Nottingham War Savings Group, the Food Office staff, women railway porters; postwomen; members of concert parties; bus conductresses and the Red Cross as well as the NAAFI. The Lord Mayor was said to be 'most anxious' of a tremendous reception for these women. The parade, beginning at 3.30 p.m. would march down Chapel Bar and into the Old Market Square where the Lord Mayor was expected to take the salute from the Council House steps. The parade would be headed by military bands, and members of the Civil Nursing Reserve and ARP would also be in attendance.

Not all women were ready and willing to get involved with war work despite it becoming compulsory in December 1941 with the National Service Act, which meant that women between the ages of 20 and 30 (later expanded to cover women between 19 and 43) had to volunteer for the armed forces or work in farming or industry.

'Women Fire Guards: More Protests', proclaimed the headline in the letters page of the *Nottingham Evening Post* 3 September 1942.

> I agree with your Hungerhill reader that women are unfit both mentally and constitutionally to do night fire watching. Married women, especially are under a terrific strain nowadays doing war work and striving to fit in housework cooking and shopping. All this does not improve the nerves and leaves little or no time for relaxation. How are we to keep healthy with this additional ordeal added to our worries? For it is an ordeal. Many women I know are trembling at the thought of it and I know that I myself will be unable to refrain from making for the nearest shelter and staying there, should a blitz occur. Of course, there are exceptions – women whose temperaments allow them to revel in dangerous jobs. Let those volunteer, and let those whose only ambition is to become mothers of healthy children stay at home safe and unafraid.

There were many different ways to volunteer during the war, not limited to the land girls or allied to the armed forces as we might naturally think of first.

The Women's Voluntary Service (WVS) recruited for all of the women's civil defence services, for example nursing, and ambulance driving. The Nottingham branch of the WVS opened in April 1939 and one of the first services initiated were three canteens situated across the city to provide refreshments for the Air Raid Precaution (ARP) volunteers and the Queen's Messengers among others. One canteen was situated at Locksley House for the city ARP report centre, with a further canteen at Victoria Station, for the use of HM Forces, opened in October 1940. Over 4,000 women were quickly recruited in Nottingham during this initial period.[7]

The WVS also administered supplies of wool for the Lord Mayor's Comforts Fund. By July 1941, over 31,500 garments had been sent to the Council House and £1,350 contributed to the Comforts Fund.

Although Nottingham was not an official reception area for those bombed out of their homes, many from other towns found their way there. These refugees were aided by the WVS in finding homes and work, more than 2,000 cases were dealt with. The WVS had a stockpile of clothes, available for distribution for those made homeless and in dire circumstances due to the hostilities.

Over 200 helpers were provided by the WVS for the rest centres in the city, and a team of three clerks was formed to assist the director of the Casualty Information Office in the event of a raid. Women were also recruited to help in emergency community feeding centres with mobile canteens and for help with emergency billeting.

Volunteers acted as drivers, transporting patients to and from hospitals and evacuating hospitals as well as driving for the regional headquarters of various ministerial departments. Other volunteers worked in the hospital supply depot and for the blood transfusion service as well as the Heathcote Street Day Nursery.

A woman named Julie was interviewed for the oral history project in the 1980s in Nottingham. She was born in 1914 and spent most of her working life in Nottingham as a domestic until her marriage in 1936 when she set up house with her husband Frank in Hucknall. Frank served in the Spanish Civil War and also in the Second World War. Julie remembers Nottingham being bombed with the nearby dairy and bakery, where Frank had worked, taking a direct hit. Although they were married in 1936 Julie considered that they only settled down in 1946, as Frank had been away fighting for so long.

Another woman who took part in the largely anonymous oral history project worked at John Player and Sons in Radford. She told the project how she had to have someone to speak for her in order to get a job there in the leaf room, on piece work. She confirmed that there were no unions in Player's when she started working there so there was no one to look out for workers' rights.

When she got married in 1937 she left Player's as, like most firms, married women were not employed. Upon her marriage she ran a shop with her husband and recalled how, during raids on Nottingham, they put all their takings in a box and went into the cellar carved into the rock underneath the house.

Changes to working patterns and practices were forced upon industry by the Second World War. Old attitudes had to be put to one side and married women were encouraged back into the workplace. Kate Albina Marshall told how she signed up at the Labour Exchange for munitions work. She was initially told that she would have to move away from Nottingham but because she had her mother to take care of, she was put into Raleigh, who had turned to war manufacturing.

Kate joined Raleigh in 1942 and worked on the conveyor belt examining parts, until the end of the war. When the war was over she went back to Ashwell's, a clothing factory.

When the Second World War began, Nancy Cook, born in Carrington, went to work at Player's, she was in her 40s at the time and her youngest child had turned 15. As soon as Nancy had been old enough to leave school, aged 14, she had gone to work, firstly in Hozene, a local factory producing sanitary products, and then to Wheldon and Wilkinson's to work as a winder, where she earned five shillings a week for five twelve-hour shifts. Unusually, as married women were not welcomed, Nancy also tells of how she worked at Lewis (later to become Meridien), an underwear manufacturer on Alfred Street, when her children were small. Nancy was responsible for winding the silk threads through the guides of the machine.

Alice, born in 1897 in Radford, told how she went to work at the Player's factory. 'It were jolly good. You went to work at eight in the morning until six at night, and on Saturday it was eight until around twelve.' Alice worked in the box-making department with a quota to be reached each day, which she said was hard work to achieve; she was paid five shillings a week. The manager of the department, one Mr Hatherley, frequently told the girls they were too slow and he could easily go out into the Market Square and get cheaper labour.

Alice still worked at Player's when the Second World War broke out and told how, when the sirens went off they all had certain jobs to do, like shutting the windows and drawing the blackout curtains for safety. She said, 'We had to go right down in the basement, right into the bowels of the earth.' One day Alice went at home at lunchtime and on her return journey, saw a fight in the sky between two planes. She was standing in the street watching the planes when a hand came on her shoulder and pulled her into the factory where she made her way to the shelter in the cellars. She hated going down into the cellars and still had bad dreams about them many years later.

Women's Groups

The National Union of Women Workers was a group of women from the middle and upper classes who did not have to go out to work. They formed themselves together in the late 1880s to try to improve the lives of women who did have to go out to work. They concentrated on the welfare of women, rather than improving women's rights as a whole. The first national conference was held in Nottingham in 1895.

These women may have found themselves in hot water had they tried to press for women's rights; many of the women were the wives and daughters of prominent business owners in the town.

In April 1918, the committee of the NUWW received a request from the Freedom League to send delegates to attend the first meeting for the Equal Pay, Equal Work campaign. The League was founded by former members of the Women's Social and Political Union who were opposed to violence and preferred peaceful protest such as non-payment of taxes. Part of their work consisted of improving women's lives and one way of doing this was by campaigning for better working conditions.

The NUWW committee decided that no delegate was to officially attend, although their reasons were not given. Despite the fight for equal pay beginning in the late 1800s, the Equal Pay Act was not passed until 1970 and finally came into force in 1975.

By 1926, the National Union of Women Workers had changed its name to the Council of Women, although their areas of work remained largely unchanged. Colonel Brook DSO MC, Chief Constable of Nottinghamshire, addressed one of their meetings on 5 December 1927. Women had begun patrols during the Great War to help the vulnerable females in the city and were now enrolled as members of the police force with corresponding powers and authority, powers which they had not held before. Two female constables had so far been appointed to the police force in Nottingham at a starting wage of sixty shillings per week, rising to eighty shillings with a six shillings a week allowance. Like men they qualified for a pension at two-thirds of their salary after thirty years' service.

These women police constables were used to take statements from women and children, as it was believed that they could get a child to talk where perhaps a man could not, or indeed when the mother had failed. They had especially distinguished themselves in the detection of female shoplifters. It was said that these constables saved the businesses around the Market Square more money than it cost to pay them.

The Nottingham Branch of the Electrical Association for Women[8] had its inaugural meeting on 24 January 1940 at the Reform Club in Victoria Street. This was not an association for women electricians as its title may suggest. The Association was set up to show women how to use, and care for, electrical appliances in the home. Lectures and demonstrations were offered on the use of kettles and refrigerators, for example, along with education and summer schools for teachers.

The EAW became a platform for women's point of view and through it much was done to improve the numbers, types and sizes of plugs and sockets installed in houses. It also helped to improve the design and construction of electric cookers.

The association's minutes recorded how the women envisaged that there may come a time when even the dishes could be washed by an electric machine.

During the fifth annual general meeting of the EAW on 23 February 1944 it was stressed that it was important to be able to purchase electricity at an economic rate after the war. It was also important to standardise plugs and sockets and increase the number installed into houses. It was envisaged that in the post-war era there would be an increase in energy-saving devices such as washing machines, washing-up machines, electric pan-scrubbers, beater-mixers, vegetable preparers and choppers. It was the aim of the EAW to see an electric refrigerator in every home.

The 1945 meeting warned that electricity should not be allowed to convert us into automatons and robots without creative powers. Electricity should be an aid to cleaner cities, smoke abatement, cleaner homes and eventually, cleaner travel by electric trains. It would take the drudgery out of housework. The electricity industry was praised in this year for producing a standard plug socket.

There were many charities and organisations in Nottingham representing women's issues and the Women's League of Nottingham was a forum, with a collection of representatives from these charitable societies coming together to support each other in their work. The first meeting of the temporary committee was held on 6 February 1891 at All Saint's Vicarage. It was resolved to approach the wives of the factory owners and manufacturers asking for their cooperation in gaining entrance to the factories in order that they may work with the women therein.

Those represented by the Women's League included Southwell House and Hope Lodge; Chaucer Street Refuge for Women;

The Servants' House; Girls' Evening Houses; the Women's Temperance Union; Women's Dining Hall and Beeston Orphanage. Lady Laura Ridding (1849–1939), founder of Southwell House and wife of the Bishop of Southwell, was asked to be the president.

The Women's League held a tea for the forewomen of factories on 11 May 1891. Around sixty women attended and some of the firms then asked the women to visit their premises and talk to their female employees. Those firms who showed interest included Messrs Dobson; Messrs Birkin and Heyman and Alexander. It was proposed that circulars were placed in the reading rooms or break rooms at the factories to try to make contact with women. The committee hoped to persuade the women to join the League or one of the associated charities. The women would then be educated in the areas of sanitation, nursing, education, and consider new opportunities. Their efforts were designed to help all classes of women but the overriding view that the woman's role in the home was of the utmost importance, still prevailed.

The National Conference of Women Workers was held in Nottingham in October 1895 and the local branch was busy most of the year producing tickets, organising the events, arranging for the press to attend and not least, arranging accommodation for the delegates attending.

Equality

An article in the *Nottingham Evening Post* of 21 March 1934 warned of the dangers of women-only schools. Dr H. Chrichton-Miller was addressing a meeting of the Women's Council to Advocate Masters for Boys. He felt that to get the requisite number of the 'right kind of men' in the future, school masters and not school mistresses should be employed. The issue was not one of cost, as women could be paid less than men for doing the same job. Some women felt the same way. Lady Oxford and Lady Asquith were reported to have said, referring to the different sense of justice that prevailed in men as opposed to women, that women would not like to be judged by a woman. It was still believed that women could not hold positions of trust or power.

In an article entitled 'Unmarried Women, A Question of the Day', (*The Nottingham Journal* 16 April 1919) Constance B. McKenzie said that when men and women are equally free they will choose companions 'purely for the love of each other'. She claimed that girls would not marry for a home and shelter in fear of being left homeless and penniless if they remained single. She said, 'when we are no longer dependent on marriage for a livelihood, we shall honour and respect men for their livelihood alone'. She went on to say that the women who remained single would be pioneers of a new type of womanhood: 'Free from responsibilities we would otherwise have taken, we may find life a wide field for exploration and a splendid great adventure.'

Not all women had such foresight, or believed in freedom for women despite having recently been granted the vote.

In *The Nottingham Journal and Express* on 29 December 1920, the writer of the column 'Woman of Today' declared that chaperoning, abandoned during the war, was making a comeback. No longer was it acceptable for women to go to the theatre or dances on their own. Parents who had allowed their daughters a certain amount of freedom during the war were reasserting their authority and insisting on chaperones.

She went on to say that many women did not have an aunt or older sister to chaperone them and relied on a professional chaperone. Such chaperones had to have tact, understanding, a keen social sense and experience. The profession was thought to be a good thing.

The suitability of women for jury service was being discussed in *The Nottingham Journal* on 24 June 1930. It was thought that only some women were suitable, the lower classes had proved themselves to be unsuitable by arguing among themselves, and middle-class and upper-class women were urged to register their willingness to serve on a jury, instead of the current arrangements where women were being compelled to serve on the jury when they were not suitable. The article, by Lilia Rose Clyna, claimed that many women had a maternal instinct that overrode the logical evidence. What if a child of theirs had found themselves in that position? Such women would claim 'not guilty', whatever the evidence, in her opinion. While there may have been some truth in this sentiment, Ms Clyna omitted to recognise the intelligence that women possessed.

Clyna further claimed that it was absurd to have spinsters as part of the jury on a divorce case. How could they possibly know the trials and tribulations, the happiness and heartbreak of marriage? 'On this count alone there would be greater wisdom in adopting the plan of registration, to those who are ready and anxious to become jury women.' She went on to say that although juries should be made up of people from all walks of life, there were thousands of women who were not suitable. She maintained that a register of volunteers would resolve all of these issues. Likewise, presumably, there were thousands of unsuitable men.

The Nottingham Evening Post of 13 April 1921, with the headline 'Back to Cheap Woman Labour', reported on the new plan for a fair and peaceful settlement of the wages issue in the engineering trade. It provoked much excitement and comment. The wages problem was described as the most 'vital and urgent' matter of the hour. Margaret Bondfield of the National Federation of Women Workers, in a letter to the *Daily News,* stated that drastic cuts in the wages of women workers would bring back the days of cheap female labour. The reduction in wages were to be linked to a reduction in the cost of living and were put forward by the Engineering Federation. The cuts would see women's wages fall by 7*s* 6*d* per week at age 21 and 11*s* 6*d* a week at age 18. The reduction was to operate until the pre-war level of the cost of living had been achieved. Bondfield stated in her letter that taking wages back to those levels was taking women back to poverty, as they had been poorly paid before the war. It was feared the sweated industry was returning.

Over the century to 1950 women's working lives had changed enormously. Their working hours had been reduced, their conditions at work improved and attempts to make their pay equal to that of a man doing the same job had been many. Not only that, many more jobs had opened up to women as a result of their efforts during two world wars and the changes made to their education. However, attitudes were slow to change and many people, including some women, still believed that a woman's place was in the home. There was still a lot of work to do in order for women to be considered equal.

CHAPTER THREE

Life on the Home Front

❖

Timeline of Statutes

1884 Matrimonial Causes Act: denied a man the right to lock up his wife because she refused sex. However, shockingly, marital rape was not made unlawful until 1994.

1857 Divorce Act: reformed divorce laws. Men could divorce women for adultery, but women had to prove bigamy, sodomy, bestiality, cruelty or long-term desertion.

1886 Maintenance of Wives Act: gave magistrates power to order maintenance be paid to deserted women.

1873 Custody of Infants Act: gave women the right to keep their children.

1895 Summary Jurisdiction Act: gave battered women a right to obtain a divorce.

1885 The Criminal Law Amendment Act: raised the age of sexual consent for women to 16 years.

At the start of our time period, 1850, the main ambition for a woman was to marry well and raise a family. As women gained other freedoms, such as more leisure time and, incrementally, the vote, their attitudes towards marriage changed, and many statutes during this 100-year period, provided protection for women.

At the start of the centenary women could sue for Breach of Promise if a man failed to fulfil his promise of marriage, implied upon becoming engaged. Being jilted could be devastating for an ex-fiancée, not only could her reputation be damaged by being labelled 'unwanted goods', but marriage was often essential for financial security and failing to secure a husband could often mean poverty. By the end of the period, and with newly gained independence, women were not outcast or shunned if they chose to remain single. However, they may have been considered to be a little odd, as it was still assumed that every woman wanted to get married.

As statutes over the century to 1950 helped to protect women and began to redress the balance of inequality, many charities worked hard to help women to improve their lives in practical ways, alongside the legislation.

Southwell House catered for women who found themselves at the mercy of the courts or in some other dire situation. The home, which opened in 1886 and eventually closed in 1982, developed from rescue and preventative work by Lady Laura Ridding and her friends, with girls living in workhouses, prisons, houses of correction or those who had been reduced to roaming the streets.

Courting and Marriage

Courtship was very different to today, not least because of the lack of social media. Nancy Cook recounted her experiences to the oral history project of the early 1980s.

Nancy worked at Wheldon and Wilkinson's as a winder from around 1913, when she met her husband, Jack. Her sister Ada, who also worked at the same factory, told her one day, 'That lad Jack Cook wants to tek you for a walk.' Nancy tells of how they went to the pictures at Boulevard Cinema. When she got home her mum was not happy. 'You bin laddin agen ant yer, yer not ode enuf to go laddin.' Nancy was 14 at the time.

This did not seem to deter Nancy who became engaged to marry Jack Cook, just before he went off to France in the Great War. When she received a telegram informing her that Jack had been injured and was in a London hospital, Nancy caught the next train to go to visit him, even though she had never been to London before and did not know her way around.

Jack recovered and returned to the Front; when he later came back on leave, Nancy said he was still covered in mud. He got on the tram with Nancy and his brother Fred and refused to pay the fare. She was embarrassed when Jack was challenged by the conductor but the other people on the tram agreed he should not have to pay as he was still a serving soldier. They had to get a special licence to get married before he went back to France after his leave. At their wedding, his sister 'got in with' Nancy's brother Richard and they later married.

Nancy proudly tells that she was the first occupant of the new council houses, in the mid-1930s, on Wendover Drive and still lived in the house at the time of the project, some forty-six years later.

Many local charities, largely run by women, helped wherever they could and often persuaded local authorities to provide help.

Emergency Aid

The files of the town clerk's office from February 1919[1] revealed a letter from Mrs W.H. Carey to the Watch Committee, which dealt with police matters, calling attention to the shortage of shelter for girls and women 'stranded' in Nottingham. She produced a list of girls who had been helped by the YWCA in January and how they were dealt with. She asked for a house, simply furnished, where twelve to fifteen girls could be accommodated each night. She said that it was dangerous to leave girls without a house and urged the Watch Committee to help.

Some of the examples she gave included the following:

Elizabeth Greinson WAAC, stranded for the night travelling home the next day – slept on the sitting room sofa.

Mrs Smith with two small children came to visit her husband in Radcliffe hospital – slept on the sofa and in the easy chair.

C.M. Tinker brought by two soldiers around 11.30 p.m. Persuaded to return to her home near Manchester the next day.

Shortly thereafter, two bedrooms were taken in a house a quarter of a mile from the YWCA, initially for a period of two weeks. Mrs Carey reports back to the committee, a few weeks later, that the house is now fully utilised. Most of the ladies used the rooms as they had missed their last train home, including Miss Cowling, going to Derby; Mrs Sewell, travelling to Lincoln and Mary Smith going to Mansfield. Others were visiting soldiers in hospital and had nowhere to stay, like Miss Leatherland visiting her brother. Occasional comments were added to the list of women – Mrs Crossley, 'not a desirable woman, addicted to drink', or Nurse Robinson missed her train to Radcliffe, she had to leave at 6 a.m., given her breakfast at 5.15 a.m., 'rather an ungrateful person'.

In late September 1919, thirty-three women were stranded in Nottingham due to the railway strike. All were accommodated and slept in the armchairs and on sofas when the beds were full. The YWCA also catered, briefly, for runaways. Mrs Davies arrived from Wales in November 1919. She had four young children with her, ranging from 4 to 9 in age. She had left home without her husband's knowledge and he was summoned to collect her and their children. An ominous note at the end of the entry reads 'the police supervised this case'.

In May 1920, two land girls, Annie and Elizabeth Maxwell, arrived in Nottingham looking for work, having just been demobbed from Grantham.

Eventually the hostel at 35 Addison Street, which had seventeen beds, was closed as the lease had expired. The hostel was moved to larger premises at Locksley House, 1 Robin Hood's Chase. With twenty-six beds and two sitting rooms, this house could accommodate many more women. Payment was required of 8*d* per night, although most of the women could only afford two-thirds of the cost. An average of 100 beds per week were occupied during 1921/22, emphasising the need for such hostels.

Unmarried women

The 1920 annual meeting of Southwell House was held in the Church Parlour at Nottingham's Albert Hall. Miss Higson gave the address on social work and praised the value of policewomen with regard to protective work among young girls during the war. An appeal was sent to the Watch Committee for policewomen to be reinstated, as the role had ceased to exist when the Great War ended.

It was recorded at this meeting that many of the girls who were helped were 16–17 years old with some as young as 14. In 1921, a total of forty-nine girls were helped after leaving prison.

Reports from 1900, when a new home was opened on Newstead Grove, North Sherwood Street, confirmed that girls helped upon release from prison did quite well, except for those girls who were victims of drink. 'They often make great promises and intend to keep them but their softened brains and weak wills prevent their doing what they could.'

Miss Fletcher, the superintendent of the home told of a success story. She got to know a girl who was in prison twelve years before on charges of theft. When the girl left prison she spent some time in Southwell House before being sent abroad in a position of trust. She had recently returned for a visit and Miss Fletcher found that she was now happily married with a baby of her own.

The report to the annual general meeting in 1901 delved into some of the reasons that the women and girls appeared at the door of Southwell House. The blame was laid at the feet of the parents who raised their children in such 'baseness' that it became natural for the children to fall into sin. 'They are so permeated with evil ideas that they flare into vice when exposed to opportunity.'

The casebook of Southwell House had many similar stories of women being imprisoned for drinking offences and subsequently being helped by Southwell House. One particular widow, aged 50, was placed, after two stints in prison, in a home for epileptic children as a needlewoman. She found that the residents needed her and she was able to help them, thus keeping her off the drink.

The story of Ellen Toley, admitted in March 1887, is particularly sad. She was dismissed from her job as a housemaid when she accidentally dropped and broke a water bottle. She was instantly dismissed without references or the pay that was owed to her. It was unlikely that she would be able to obtain a new position without references from a previous employer; out of desperation she then tried to drown herself in the River Trent. She was transferred to the Lenton orphanage from Southwell House.

Sarah Ann Strutt was also admitted to Southwell House in 1887. She was taken to the home by her sister Mrs Jenny Coleman, who had also been through the house in her youth. Sarah had two children and had been unfaithful to her husband. One child was with its father and one with Mrs Coleman. She did not want to go back to her husband, but did want to get away from the man she had been 'sinning' with. She was eventually sent to the House of Good Shepherd in Shepherd's Bush and from there went into service.

Many women of the middle or upper classes were aware of, and grateful for, their privilege. Marianne Mason,[2] (1845–1932) was the daughter of a landowner with property on the edge of Sherwood Forest. Her grandfather was the former rector of Whitwell in Derbyshire and she spent many of her days helping the poor in her neighbourhood, caring for the sick and also taught in Sunday school; she took the boys and girls out for walks in the woods whenever possible, describing the local children as delightful and intelligent. Her mother and grandmother had provided nursing services for the neighbourhood and Marianne followed suit, recalling a time when she helped an old, dying, woman at Whitwell. The woman had been ill for a while and no one would go near her because she was in such a poor condition. Marianne nursed her for the final six weeks of her life.

During an outbreak of scarlet fever she took supplies to villagers and disinfected their cottages herself. During an outbreak of smallpox Marianne held a vaccine party in one of the cottages and was vaccinated eight times herself to show the women there was nothing to be afraid of. She then helped to administer the vaccine some of the women herself.

Marianne also worked with the Boarding Out Committee, which arranged for children in need to be placed with families who were paid for their care, rather than be sent to the workhouse. Marianne also visited foster parents in the parish and recalled visiting one such foster mother, from a very respectable family, in Ambleside. The woman had two girls staying with her and had been given money for clothes for the girls, but it was obvious that they had not had any new garments. When the ladies from the committee visited they found the 5-year-old black and blue from a beating; the children were withdrawn from that particular home.

Although Marianne was very much a hands-on, practical helper she also raised these issues and campaigned for improvements wherever possible and gave evidence to the Royal Commission on Poor Law in 1906 about how epidemics had disrupted children's education in the district.

Marianne organised someone from the Girls' Friendly Society to visit all of the girls who were boarded out or in the workhouse. She had to obtain the leave of the Board of Guardians for the area in order for these visits to be made. Marianne took good care to make friends with the chairman of each board to make this permission easier to obtain. Only the Basford Board of Guardians refused to engage with her, which she put down to 'unreasoning jealousy of their little authority'.

These visiting ladies had no power within each union, even if they found mistreatment or abuse of the children. At that time the Relieving Officer, or Medical Officer for the union held that power. She felt that some of the Relieving Officers, who were male, defended these foster women, even if there was clear abuse, as it would be seen as an attack on their authority for someone else to interfere. It was also thought to be fairly easy for the foster mothers to put on a good front when the inspections were made by the board officers, whereas continuous visitation would make it more difficult for problems to be hidden. Her desire above all things was the protection of the children.

Marianne's first speech was to a meeting in Nottingham in 1882, at time when it was still quite unusual for women to speak in public. They were thought of as brazen or seeking notoriety. Through this speech Marianne became acquainted with Mr Morley, Education Inspector of Poor Law Schools. She went on to become the first woman to speak at a Poor Law Conference, held in London where she spoke about the link between the Girls' Friendly Society and boarding-out of children and how the two should be working together.

In 1885, Marianne was appointed to inspect boarding-out beyond the union (a combination of parishes for the purposes of relief), where children had been fostered by mothers who lived outside the union to which the children belonged. This was a full twelve years before a woman was appointed to inspect Poor Law schools (schools set up by the Board to cater for poor children. These were often part of, or adjacent to, the union workhouse).

This fact surprised Marianne as she felt that firstly, a woman's perceptions were keener than a man's, especially when it came to children, and secondly, that household affairs and the care of children were the domain of women, not men.

A foster parent had to sign an undertaking as to the conditions under which he or she was to receive and treat the child. This included allowing an inspection. However, the inspections were only cursory and therefore not effective, in Marianne's view.

On 9 March 1883, Marianne went to see Sir John Hibbert, the Parliamentary Secretary of the School Board. She persuaded him that inspectors should be women. He asked her to take the job. This was not what she had intended and she was not keen on the idea of travelling all over England and Wales. However, she thought she ought to take the post for the sake of the children and carried out the work for three years before she was officially appointed by the then Conservative government.

The appointment of a woman was so novel and so risky, that initially it was for three months only. During that time Marianne had to inspect as many children and their homes as possible and report on the system itself, each individual child and each home. The salary was £400 per year, as Marianne herself said, 'the valuation of a pioneer woman'. She claimed that she carried out her inspections in the spirit of finding out whether everything was in order, even though on some occasions this was not what she found. She felt that the whole weight of future women inspectors depended upon her.

In 1889, she helped to draft the new orders for care of children. Women now had to be included on every Boarding Out committee. Each committee was obliged to inform the board of any death, resignation or removal of its members, a direct result of Marianne's findings in the initial three months' work. These orders were further revised in 1903, and included a limit on the numbers of children in one home; a ban on placing a child with anyone who had been convicted of a crime; not placing a child in a public house or licensed premises, and a ban on foster parents insuring the children for death or illness.

The objections to women being on these committees were many and varied, aside from viewing the women as interfering in matters that were above their intelligence. They included arguments that it was improper for women to sit at a board with men and hear subjects discussed in mixed company, which were not fit for feminine ears.

Marianne gave evidence before seven committees or commissions including the House of Lords Select Committee (HOLSC) on Poor Law and Relief of Distress in 1888; HOLSC on Infant Life Protection in 1896; the Parliamentary Committee on Infant Life Protection of 1908; Committee on Poor Law Schools 1896 and Royal Commission on Care and Control of the Feeble Minded.

Her practical work and political determination helped improve the lives of many children and to safeguard their welfare.

Attitudes were slow to change and many men continued to resist change.

Bernard Johnson BA, a confirmed bachelor and organist at Nottingham Albert Hall, addressed a meeting of the National Council for Women Nottingham and Nottinghamshire Branch[3] on 14 January 1929. He made various claims about women which could very well explain why he was unmarried. He said that women were deficient in logic as a rule, but they made up for it by a certain quality that could be called 'courage', although he preferred to call it 'nerve'. He thought that sisters were of 'an advantage to a man', but there was a 'certain type of woman it was a misery to go shopping with: the maximum amount of trouble was given, with the minimum amount of money spent, and the shop turned upside down.' He reported to the women that it was not uncommon for Nottingham people to be late for concerts. A woman would make her way to her seat, sweeping off coats, hats, and scarves onto the floor with perfect 'sang froid. The man follows behind, the picture of abject misery. This is woman's nerve', he claimed. He also stated that if there is one thing he loathed it was lipstick!

Housing and Home Conditions

The women of the NCW continued to support women's causes and provide help to local women wherever possible. In 1929, the annual meeting was addressed by Dr Dorothea Mann who spoke about infant mortality. She stated that the infantile death rate had gone down by two-thirds, but the death rate for mothers had hardly gone down at all. Fathers should be educated in how to take care of their wives following confinement and the branch should agitate for better houses, more baths, better lighting and better sanitation of all kinds. She said pioneer work had been done by Dr Sarah Gray, the first woman doctor in the city which made it much easier for other women doctors here.

The newspaper report following the annual general meeting reported that Canon Geoffrey Gordon, vicar of St Mary's Nottingham, also spoke about the health of the people. He claimed that conditions were over-crowded and high moral standards could not be expected when young people of both sexes had to share a bedroom.

Nottingham Housing Improvement Association was trying to tackle the problem of the slums, so often mentioned as the root of problems ranging from health to sexual matters. The association was demonstrating to local landlords that decent housing could be provided and that they would still get a good return on their money. As a result, hospitals, asylums and prisons would all save money. The pulling-down of slum housing was said to be making matters worse for the poorer people. To tackle this, the Housing Association was buying houses and reconditioning them to then rent them out to the displaced families from the slums. Thirty-one houses had been purchased and renovated in 1928.

A.F. Crewdson, chairman of the Housing Committee of the Corporation, said that since the Great War, 6,000 new houses had been built. They were hoping that the recently built two-bedroom flats would ease the situation. Lady Maud Rolleston, wife of a South Notts Hussars officer, Sir Lancelot Rolleston, commented that her dogs lived in better accommodation than some of the houses she had seen in Bulwell.

Major T.C. Howitt gave the address at the February 1930 meeting. Some thirty estates had now been erected or were in the process of being erected. During 1928/29, a house had been completed every 1¾ hours on a Nottingham estate. The houses were being let at 6s 4d per week. The houses were costing the extraordinarily low (according to the major) figure of £295 to construct. Not a single house was being erected in Nottingham without a bathroom or hot water supply.

'Nottingham Housing Estate as Complete Social Centre,' announced the headline in *The Nottingham Journal* on 26 October 1946. Three thousand houses were to be built at Bilborough and Strelley and had been planned as a complete neighbourhood unit for the expected 10,000 residents. The facilities were planned to include a 70-acre school site, a park, a playing fields extension; half a dozen sites for nursery schools and business; and provisions for bungalows for old people. There was also planned a social centre where there would be shops, a church, a community centre, a cinema, health centre and library. The main artery would be a road named Bracebridge Drive. The plans were revealed by Councillor G.H. Wigman, vice chairman of the Nottingham Housing Committee.

Married Women

Although women were always referred to as 'the wife of' so and so, rather than having their own identity, many of them did have lives of their own, within their marriages, even if they did not earn their own income. One such woman was Lady Maud Rolleston of Watnall Hall. She was married in 1882 and followed her husband to South Africa during the Boer War in 1901. Once there, she set up nursing facilities for her husband's regiment and later for men from any regiment in need of nursing and rest, taking premises and rallying the other wives and residents of the town of her class to help fund and run the home.

During the Great War, Lady Maud was the organiser and secretary of Nottinghamshire Soldiers and Sailors Families' Association, raising over £80,000 over the four-year period. She became a Justice of the Peace in 1921.

Lady Maud worked constantly for women's issues, particularly those of working women. She was described by her friends as a keen and uncompromising suffragist. She was involved in Southwell House rescue home and was a trustee of the Abel Collins charity, helping to provide homes for the elderly. Lady Maud was also president of the Nottingham and Nottinghamshire branch of the National Council for Women in 1947.

The Nottingham Female Home[4] on Great Alfred Street was set up, with the help of Lady Maud, to provide a home and training for 'penitent' females before sending them home to their friends. They would also try to put others in a position which would enable them to recover their 'lost character' and regain their place in society.

In 1892, the first women Poor Law Guardians were elected in Nottingham. These four women became members of the Southwell House Committee as part of their work.

At a meeting of Southwell House committee[5] in March 1917, the Canon of Southwell spoke of the good work that the homes were doing. He was concerned about how much the house was needed as 'our young girls appear to have lost their heads', and that these girls were extraordinarily independent of any control. In 1915, Southwell House had helped 128 women and girls. In 1916, that number had risen to 213. The canon also commented that employment was difficult and thieving was on the increase.

Although it was beneficial to identify the issues, it was quite something else to be able to find a solution. This did not stop the women from trying.

Health Education

Edward Seaton, Medical Health for Nottingham 1873–83[6] said: 'It is on the lives of infants that unhealthy influences have their deadliest effects.' Sir George Newman, England's First Chief Medical Officer of Health thought that many infant deaths must be preventable and it was important to discover how these deaths could be prevented. Postnatal childhood killers of the time were epidemic diarrhoea and enteritis, often exacerbated by respiratory diseases such as pneumonia and bronchitis. Respiratory diseases as well as measles and whooping cough are affected by poor diet, overcrowding and poor housing conditions. Contemporaries believed that one of the most influential factors on infant deaths was the mother, who would be blamed for going out to work, leaving her child with unsuitable childminders and not providing a decent home in which the child could flourish.

As there was no welfare system at this time, women would have little choice in the decision to stay at home or to work.

A campaign was launched to give women an education in mothercraft to teach them about nutrition and hygiene. Initially, women were seen by lady health visitors or at clinics. At the beginning of the 1900s, Medical Health Officer for Nottingham, Phillip Boobbyer, conducted a survey to see how prevalent breastfeeding was in the city. Over half of those interviewed said they did, or would, breastfeed their babies. Boobbyer then set up the Mothers and Babies Welcome in 1908.

For many women breastfeeding was not an option, sometimes because the women had to go out to work and leave their babies with relatives or friends and sometimes because the milk these undernourished, overworked women could produce was not good enough. Even so, not breastfeeding a baby was seen as a failure on the mother's part. The alternatives, cow's milk or milk substitutes, were full of dangers with unhygienic bottles and adulterated products. Other liquid pulps, such as malt biscuits mixed with milk that mothers used, were frequently indigestible and introduced contaminants to the baby's system. Raising children was fraught with danger.

Many mothers used condensed milk, which was generally used in the household, but was unsuitable for babies. Female sanitary inspectors were employed to visit the homes of new mothers in poor areas to advise them on feeding.

The highest rates of mortality occurred in heavily populated areas such as St Ann's and The Exchange. It was noted that these were also the ones that continued to use pail closets. Rates of mortality decreased from 1920 when the use of pail closets was abandoned in Nottingham. Hot summers made the conditions worse and there was a clear link between the number of hot, dry days and the number of infant deaths. This had all but disappeared by 1926 when the pail closets had been removed.

Marriage and Divorce

'Equal rights for Men and Women – Sweeping changes to Divorce Law' declared the *Nottingham Evening Post* on 12 November 1912. The Divorce Commission was discussing proposed amendments which, if acted upon, would be a revolution of the divorce law. These amendments included decentralisation of court sittings so poor people could have their cases heard locally. Additional grounds were introduced – including desertion for three years; incurable insanity after five years of confinement; habitual drunkenness for three years after separation; and a commutable death sentence. All divorce and matrimonial cases were to be heard before a judge alone, no longer requiring a jury, which was traditionally men only. The most important recommendation was to amend the law 'so as to place the two sexes on an equal footing as regards the grounds on which divorce may be obtained'. The Commission went on to say that this was because when two different standards exist the lower is usually accepted for both sexes. There were objections to the reform, most generally from the English Church Union who claimed the country would be in uproar with the recommendations and they undermined family values.

Prior to these recommendations a man could divorce a woman on the grounds of adultery. A woman had a higher burden of proof to maintain if she wanted a divorce. Crucially, children of the marriage would be the property of the husband following a divorce until the 1873 Custody of Infants Act. Even after that time, women continued to lose their children in divorce because courts viewed the husband as more financially able to look after them.

Breach of promise to marry actions were open to women if men had promised to marry them and then changed their minds. During the early part of the twentieth century fewer actions were brought as, even if successful, damages had been decreasing, with some women only being awarded £2 or £3. A woman's reputation was at stake if a suitor declined to marry her. This would often deter future suitor, leaving the woman adrift both financially and socially. As women's rights and freedoms grew, loss of reputation was less financially devastating.

Occasionally, a court would be more sympathetic to a woman's position. In 1938, Elsie Jessie Moore brought an action against Sidney Ernest Legg. They had been courting for six years and engaged for two when he broke the engagement. It was claimed in court that this was due to the influence of his family and his mother in particular. The jury had to come to a decision as to when the engagement was terminated and whether it was mutual. Finally they reached the conclusion that it was Ernest who broke it off and Elsie was awarded £17 10s.

Marriage was seen as an achievement for women, although for many it was a disappointment.

The Nottingham Journal of 11 September 1929 reported on the court case of a young Nottingham woman who was married at the age of 17. Kathleen Flora Johnson of 11 Bathley Street, The Meadows, stated in court, upon her application for a separation order on the grounds of desertion, that her parents had not given her the freedom she desired so she decided to get married. By her first anniversary she had realised, as had her husband, Edwin William Johnson of 152c Bluebell Hill, that they did not love each other. They talked of separation until they were both persuaded by friends and relatives that having a baby would end their troubles.

In a letter written by Kathleen and published in a well-known journal, she admitted that having a child was a mistake. She had never wanted a child but hoped and believed, as her advisors had said, that it would improve her relationship. Now the couple found themselves in a worse situation. Neither spouse loved the other but both adored their child. They lived a life of unhappiness for the sake of the child. Neither wanted to deprive the child of the other parent. In her letter Kathleen said, 'I do not think a girl needs motherhood until she has explored and experienced every other aspect of life open to her. If, like myself, she has motherhood thrust at her, then she is not capable of enjoying or doing justice to what should be God's gift.'

The court ordered that the case be adjourned for three months to give this couple a chance of 'making the best of it'. It is unclear what the court expected to happen in those three months or what was expected to change. It is unclear whether the couple stayed together after the three-month period.

Hard fought-for birth control had been granted to women during the period 1850–1950 and, together with education in health and mothercraft and improved housing, women's lives had been enhanced. Marriage laws had been revolutionised, giving women more rights than ever before, even being allowed to keep their children upon the dissolution of their marriages. A woman no longer had to rely on a man for financial security as more and more women joined the workforce. Unfortunately, attitudes towards women were extremely slow to change. Many men, and indeed women, believed their best aim in life should be to find a good husband. Only over a great number of years do attitudes finally change.

CHAPTER FOUR

Health and Welfare Issues

❖

Timeline of Statutes

1864 Contagious Diseases Act (also 1866 and 1869): allowed women to be detained and forcibly examined for venereal diseases.

1886 Repeal of the Contagious Diseases Acts.

1902 Midwives Act: formalised midwife services, introducing training and a governing body in the Central Midwives Board.

1918 Maternity and Child Welfare Act: local authorities had to provide services to improve women's health, including creche facilities for working mothers.

1930 National Birth Control Council (NBCC): between 1921, when Marie Stopes opened the first birth control clinic in London, and 1930 five separate birth control societies were formed to open clinics around the country. These amalgamated in 1930 to form the Council.

1939 Family Planning Association: became the new name for the NBCC and pressured for post-natal care and contraception.

1946 Family Allowance: first paid to families.

1961 Contraception: the contraceptive pill became available on prescription.

1967 Medical Termination of Pregnancy: legalised abortion on medical grounds.

1974 – Free contraception: made available via General Practitioners.

In the 1850s and up to the early twentieth century, infant mortality was high due to, among other factors, lack of education for new mothers, and the poor state of their housing. Much work was carried out in educating women and providing services especially for women's health care needs. Midwifery was formalised during this century which also brought the National Health Service ensuring treatment was available for everyone, not just those with money.

Health and Maternity

The Poor Law Amendment Act of 1834 brought in a network of Poor Law Unions, each one run by a Board of Guardians and administered by a body of paid officials. These unions had responsibility for orphaned children, the elderly, disabled and mentally ill, as well as the sick and unemployed. In November 1856[1] 129 people were admitted to the Nottingham Union Workhouse. Of these seventy-one were women, thirty-eight of whom were destitute; seven had venereal disease; four were ill; three were pregnant and the remainder had been deserted by husbands, or had mothers who were in the infirmary or in prison. All these women were from poor backgrounds, generally with no other means of financial or emotional support.

These workhouse infirmaries gradually developed into public hospitals. The Basford Poor Law Infirmary became the Highbury Vale Hospital, for instance.

The need for the specialised treatment of women was recognised in the mid 1870s and two Nottingham hospitals for women were founded. The Castle Gate Hospital for the Diseases of Women was founded in 1875 and the Samaritan Hospital for Women opened on Raleigh Street in 1885. These hospitals depended largely on voluntary subscriptions and legacies supplemented by patients' fees, when those patients could afford to pay.

Castle Gate had twenty-two beds and over 1,000 outpatients annually. The Castle Gate and Samaritan hospitals combined in 1929 into the Women's Hospital in Peel Street which remained open until 1981.

The involvement of local authorities with public health and welfare began with Victorian sanitary reforms. The focus initially was on attempting to improve drainage and water supplies along with changes to unhealthy, back to back slum housing. Dr Boobbyer, Nottingham's Medical Officer for Health 1889–1929, was an advocate for change in this area. By the turn of the century the focus had shifted towards treating specific diseases such as tuberculosis, diptheria and scarlet fever, and on reducing infant mortality.

Initiatives stemmed from the Notification of Births (Extension) Act 1915 and the Maternity and Child Welfare Act of 1918. Local authorities acquired new responsibilities for the supervision of nursing and expectant mothers and the care of infants.

These new responsibilities saw the employment of health visitors and midwives, the regulation of milk supplies and the introduction of welfare clinics. These activities were overseen by the Maternity and Child Welfare Committee.

One lady, who chose to remain anonymous, took part in the oral history project in the 1980s. Born in 1905, she told how she arrived at Nottingham General Hospital in 1924 as a student nurse. The salary was £20 per year for a trainee rising to £30 for a third-year nurse, including board and lodging but not including the uniform. The nurses were not allowed out after 8 p.m., save for one night a week when they could stay out until 10 p.m. They had one day per month off, which was not unusual in its time, but is out of kilter with today's expectations.

Two months of training school, studying anatomy and physiology, with lectures and practical demonstrations, was followed by three months on a medical ward, three months on a surgical ward, three months on a children's ward and three months on light duty. As junior nurses, the women were expected to clean the sluice room and the bathrooms as well as sweeping and dusting.

When she had completed three years at the hospital this nurse was sent to Leeds for midwifery training. In 1930 she became a ward sister. This particular woman also helped to set up the Pay Bed Ward of the hospital ready for opening on 1 May 1938. Beds cost four guineas a week, eleven guineas if you had a single room on the top floor. This ward was separate from the main hospital and was funded completely by subscription. One bed was always reserved and not in use for the general public. It was labelled Mrs FOTH (Friends of the Hospital), and was reserved for the most generous benefactors.

The average hospital stay was three weeks and bills were capped at £30, including surgeon and anaesthetic fees. Patients came from a range of backgrounds, from local aristocracy to fairground people.

Fundraising events for the hospital were well attended and those at the Harvest Festival brought in a lot of food for the patients. Some wards were named after benefactors who had donated generously for example the Shipstone Ward. Sir Julian Cahn (a prominent Nottingham furniture supplier) donated all the furniture and bedding for several wards.

During the Second World War, patients had to be moved into the basement on more than one occasion, for safety during a bombing raid. The Co-operative Bakery suffered a hit one night, and many patients arrived at the hospital shortly thereafter, with burns injuries.

This one ward continued to operate as it always had until the nurse's retirement in 1967, despite the NHS taking over most hospitals.

The second interviewee on this topic, Miss Denman, was born in 1910. She arrived at the General Hospital in 1930 for her four years' training. After qualifying she specialised on the men's accident ward where she dealt mainly with bone injuries and head injuries.

During the Second World War, Miss Denman experienced the arrival of convoys of soldiers coming in from various ports. Ambulances would meet the patients at the train stations and ferry up to thirty soldiers from each train straight over to the hospital. Penicillin was reserved for the use of troops only. The war was the first time that Miss Denman remembered being introduced to antibiotics, which were manufactured locally by Boots.

She told how the NHS gradually brought many changes, including pay rises, to the wards. Miss Denman also recalled how the equipment they were using improved once the NHS came into being.

The sixty-first annual meeting of the Nottingham and District Nursing Association (1936) was held at 36 Regent Street Nottingham with the Marchioness of Titchfield installed as president. The vice presidents list reads like a 'who's who' for Nottingham at that time and included Lady Maud Rolleston, Lady Henry Bentinck, Lady Seely, Lady Trent and Mrs J.D. Player. The Patrons were the Duchess of Portland and the Countess of Manvers. These were busy times for the Nursing Association with nurses having visited 1,305 cases the previous year, with a total of 42,884 visits; 1936 showed an increase of 2,000 visits on the previous year. Two of the association's nurses were permanently based at John Player and Sons. They had applied 10,043 dressings in Number 1 Factory (by Nurse Shuker) and 7,053 dressings in Number 2 Factory (by Nurse Bell). Twelve patients were visited in their own homes.

In December 1936, the association had one superintendent; fifteen staff nurses and one temporary nurse. These nurses were funded by public contributions including large amounts from J.D. Player and Mrs J.D. Player and James Forman. In addition, payments of £273 17s 8d had been received from grateful patients towards the cost of their care.

Donations of clothing and food were also received by the association for distribution to the patients as necessary but especially during the winter months.

Only two years later, in 1938, the number of visits had risen to 44,983. The figures continued to be high, even during the war years of 1939–45. In 1942, Miss Eldred resigned as the superintendent, having worked for the association for thirty-one years.

In addition to the nursing association, there were various charities who provided nursing. The Abel Collins Almshouses[2] had a nursing committee to look after the inhabitants of the almshouses. On 20 July 1910, a meeting was held to select a nurse for the residents of the almshouses and to make arrangements for her housing. Present at the meeting were Messrs E.R. Smith, F.R. Radford and Miss Haywood. Lady Maud Rolleston had declined to join this particular committee due to her workload.

Plans had been submitted by the charity's surveyor for the erection of a house for the nurse on the south side of the chapel in Park Street at an estimated cost of £300. The following meeting, in September 1910, revealed that tenders had been received for the building work. They ranged from £427 to £470. The lowest tender, from Fish and Son, was accepted. The ladies, Miss Haywood and now Mrs Brownsword, were tasked with furnishing the house and drawing up a list of articles required with a view to obtaining tenders from the leading furnishers.

Only in October 1911 was the decision taken to advertise for a resident nurse. The applications were left to the ladies to sift through and a shortlist was to be given to the meeting in November, with six of the applicants being invited for interview. The ladies were given a budget of £80 to purchase the necessary furnishings for the house.

The November meeting resolved to offer the position of nurse to Esther Read, aged 43, who was at that time living in Birmingham. The minute book shows, in February 1913, that Esther's employment was terminated by the charity due to her 'continued inability' to discharge her duties. An account of £1 19s for damage to Nurse Read's dress by fire was referred to the fire insurance company. The minutes do not record how Nurse Read's dress came to be damaged by fire, or why she was unable to discharge her duties. Nurse Read applied to the committee for compensation and this was passed to the insurance company after consultation with solicitors.

At the meeting in April 1913 the solicitor was present and the compensation claim was discussed. It was decided to arrange for a payment to her of no more than £100, provided all of her Nottingham debts were paid and subject to the approval of the Charity Commission. There was clearly a lot more to the story than one burned dress! Nurse Read was replaced by Nurse Constance Ellen Taylor of Peterborough who appeared to be safe from fire risks.

Several other points of interest in the minutes include the installation of wireless sets in 1929 and a telephone for the nurse in 1937. When the Carrington Street area was being redeveloped, around 1938, the residents were moved to Friar Lane and to new houses on Derby Road in Beeston.

During the Second World War, air raid shelters were built at the Friar Lane and Derby Road premises. The patients' book for the period shows that most people were treated for minor injuries or removed to Bagthorpe Hospital if their illness/injury was more severe.

Southwell House, set up in 1886 by the Bishop of Southwell and his wife, continued its work over the years and its patrons revelled in its success. In 1923, the annual meeting in the Exchange Building was told that preventative cases in the year had almost doubled, but during the previous six months, there had been a decrease in the number of women and girls in local prisons.

During 1923, a new home for the unmarried mother had been opened by the charity at 49 Leenside and the charity had obtained the help of 'a woman whose practical sympathies were wholly on the side of the bottom dog.'[3] Mrs H.A.L. Fisher of London, who gave the address at the annual meeting, declared that it was impossible to cure an evil by keeping it secret.

The acute shortage of midwives during the war was exacerbated by the increased birth rate in 1946. Equally in 1946, midwives and health visitors were encouraged to continue their efforts to ensure a large take up of the foods recommended for nursing and expectant mothers: milk, orange juice and cod liver oil. Lower prices were charged to those women and if they were on national assistance the recommended foods would be free. The shortage of midwives meant that a number of cases had to be admitted to the city hospital. It was proposed that mother and baby be sent home three days after giving birth.

Some of the midwives used their own cars or motorcycles to carry out their visits and the council agreed to pay them an allowance to cover their costs. In 1948, the eighteen midwives employed by the council attended 6,732 live births and 143 stillbirths. Health visitors during the same year made a total of 23,870 visits to children under 1 year and 18,363 visits to children between 1 and 5 years.

Two residential nurseries had long stay beds for children. The Central Home on Hartley Road had twenty beds for 3- to 5-year-olds and Beechwood Nursery had thirty-five beds for birth to 3-year olds. There were fifty-one home helps who assisted at forty-one confinements that year.

Further changes for the midwives were announced in October 1946 in a Central Midwives Board circular. A national uniform was proposed, with a hat and cape bearing buttons with the letters SCM. The proposed uniform was to be displayed at the Nursing and Midwife's exhibition at Seymour Hall Seymour Place W1 on 21–25 October of that year. These uniforms were to be compulsory from 1 February 1947 and could only be obtained from approved contractors, all of whom were in London.

In August 1949, National Insurance Maternity Benefits were announced. A £4 maternity grant was allowed for every child born, £8 for twins, to be claimed up to three months after the birth. A 20s a week attendance allowance was given for four weeks after the birth and had to be claimed within twenty-eight days of the birth.

The end of the war had proved a very busy time for local midwives and the new National Health Service.

Causes of Health Issues

In 1926, the Bishop of Southwell reflected that the average age of the girls at Southwell House homes had fallen to 17 and lamented that girls had moved away from being controlled, somewhat earlier in life. Just one year later it was claimed in the *Nottingham Guardian* that the majority of the work being carried out at the Leenside home was dealing with drunkenness among quite young girls. How to prevent such drunkenness was a 'trying and worrying' problem. The mayor commented that he had seen the behaviour himself when he sat on the magistrates' bench. He told of a widow, aged 28, who had five young children, being drunk in St Peter's Square due to the burden of her work. The Sheriff went on to say that no doubt poor housing added to the problem.

It should be remembered that this was less than ten years after the Great War and many slums still existed within the city.

The bishop took up his theory, that lack of control of young girls led to mischief, once again in 1929 at the annual meeting. He said that lessening of parental control giving girls greater freedom and independence made rescue work extraordinarily difficult. The working girl now had more economic freedom than her sisters ten years before. He went on to say that unless the whole question of bad housing, underpaid labour, and ignorance or wrong-teaching about sex matters was tackled, progress would be slow.

The acquisition of the motor car by local men also seemed to be part of the problem in 1931 when Alderman A. Pollard presided over the annual meeting of Southwell House, and said that innocent girls and young women were being trapped by men in cars. In 1932, the work of Southwell House gradually became known as moral welfare work, rather than rescue and preventative work. The annual report revealed that 186 girls had been helped by Southwell House and these were girls whose upbringing and home surroundings would have made it well-nigh impossible for them to keep straight without the influence of Southwell House staff.

Dr Herbert Gray spoke at the annual meeting on 29 March 1933 at the Albert Hall Institute Lecture Hall. He also complained that pay was very low, girls had to work long hours and their environment was poor. This left them wanting change and excitement, which led to trouble, he said. So long as men regarded women as playthings and pretended to offer love when they offered nothing of the sort, life would be hard for girls. He claimed that, in the vast majority of cases, the root of the problem was the absence of true sex education. To emphasise his point he reported that eighty-nine girls and eight babies had been accommodated during the year to the meeting. The home was in overdraft with the bank and more funds were urgently needed.

The meeting in 1935 followed much the same theme. The speaker, Dr Henry Mosley, Bishop of Southwell, confirmed that there were fewer ill houses and brothels in the city at that time than in 1885. However, the advent of the motor car meant 'this evil was to be found most flagrantly in the lanes and byways of the country'. Villagers had told the bishop that on Sundays, cars were driven by men out to the villages and girls were taken out in the cars into the lanes surrounding the villages. He continued,

> So long as society tolerates the notion that that which is pardonable in a man is unpardonable in a woman, we shall not make effective progress. Men will be what women expect of them and the actual influence in this matter lies with women, he claimed. If the women of England would once make up their mind that they would have patience no longer with this horrible double standard, the double standard would very quickly go.

These same problems continued throughout the decade and in 1938 the keynote speaker, Mrs Rawlinson, wife of the Bishop of Derby, claimed that the courts were crowded with young people for three reasons: firstly, the 'emancipation of women in large cities; secondly, pillion riding; and thirdly, young people of 12 or 13 years of age with knowledge of contraception'.

The annual report stated that the accommodation at Southwell House was now too cramped. They had decided to pull down the old cottage and rebuild to include a clubroom where girls could bring their friends, a new laundry and drying room. The scheme would cost around £1,650, two-thirds of which had already been pledged.

The speech at the annual meeting in March 1939 was again given by Dr Herbert Gray. He expanded on his theory from previous meetings, claiming that the worst possible training for life was to live in a home where husband and wife were making each other miserable. If they were unhappy and broke out into 'storm tempers and passions, and the whole place was upset, then terrible harm was done to young life'. He said that people should not be allowed to marry unless they were told what marriage meant and how to make it successful.

The Marchioness of Titchfield, speaking at the 1941 annual meeting confirmed that the work of Southwell House was becoming increasingly difficult in the face of the new temptations given to girls under wartime conditions. Many girls were then being remanded to Southwell House instead of being sent to prison.

In May 1944, the annual meeting was held in at the YMCA Hall. Bishop Heywood, former Bishop of Southwell, spoke of the spread of venereal disease and how he believed that the moral issue should not be raised because people would be less likely to go to clinics for

CHAPTER ONE

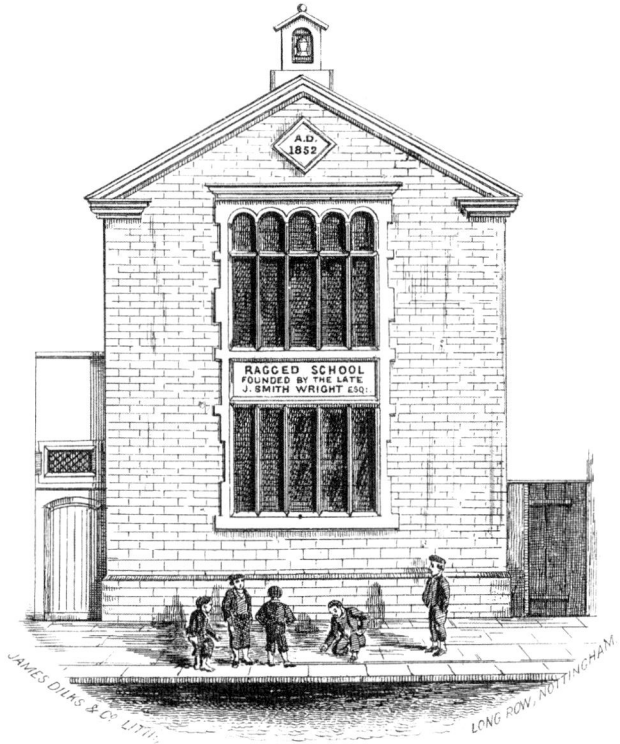

Right: *The Ragged School on Glasshouse Street, founded in 1852, where children of the working class were provided free education.*

Below: *An unknown School in Nottingham circa 1890. The class size is large with a curious repeat picture of swans.*

CHAPTER TWO

Above: *Lace workers at home on Knotted Alley in Narrowmarsh. These ladies would mend any imperfections in the pieces of lace. Intricate work.*

Left: *The Lamberts were the owners of a lace and hosiery factory on Talbot Street. This young lady was one of their maids and worked long hours in the houseful for little financial reward. Circa 1901.*

Workers leaving the Players factory at the end of their shift. 1920s.

Not everyone was pleased with the inception of the Women's Land Army in the Great War. This picture is from 1917.

CITY OF NOTTINGHAM.

AIR RAID PRECAUTIONS.

THIS IS TO CERTIFY

That   Cicely Sleaford (Communications Warden)

has attended a Course of Lectures in Air Raid Precautions and First Aid for Air Raid Casualties, and has satisfied the Examiner.

CIVIL DEFENCE HEADQUARTERS,
GOLDSMITH STREET,
NOTTINGHAM.

DATE 12th May, 1943.

Lt.-Commander, A.R.P. CONTROLLER.

Cicely Sleaford's Air Raid Precaution training completion certificate.

Women Air Raid Wardens World War Two.

Above: *Young women in the Player's cigarette factory, building cigarette boxes. 1920s.*

Left: *Lady Laura Ridding 1849 – 1939 Socialist, suffragist and the wife of the Bishop of Southwell.*

Chestnut Grove Children's Hospital 1925, Parents were not allowed to visit their children in hospital for fear of upsetting the children and hampering their recovery.

Lewis Square 1930s. The yard and toilet facilities were shared by all of the occupants. There were many of these yards around Nottingham until the slum clearances of the 1930s when new estates were built, most with indoor plumbing.

An aerial view of the Beechdale Estate nearing completion in the late 1920s.

CHAPTER FOUR

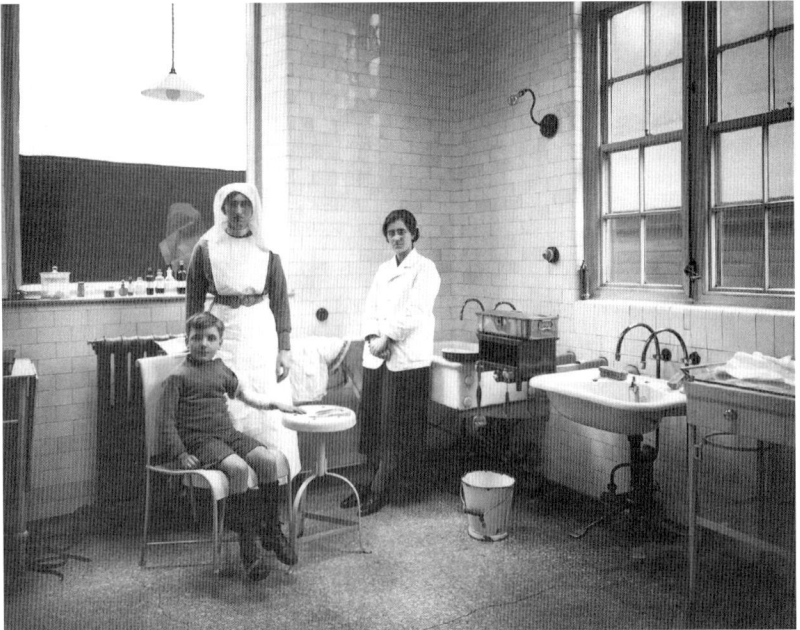

Treatment Room at the Nottingham Dispensary 1926.

Above: *The Prince of Wales visit to open the new nurses home at the General Hospital Park Row.*

Right: *Collins Almshouses off Friar Lane Nottingham. They were demolished in 1956 aroudn the time of the Maid Marian Way road development scheme.*

Tel' 64285.

**THE SHERWOOD RISE
MATERNITY and MEDICAL HOME,**

Principal; Miss R. Marshall, S. R. N., S. C. M.,

Fees from 3½ Gns. to 7 Gns.

1, Herbert Road,
Sherwood Rise,
Nottingham.

No 36. & 37. Trolley Bus,

15 - 9 - 1938

Mrs. *atter*

To Professional Services

1 week @ 3½ gns.	£	3 - 13 - 6
1 week @ 3½ gns only		3 - 3 - 6
Theatre & Laundry fee		1 0 - 0
		7 - 17 - 0

Received c. Thanks

21 - 9 - 38

R. Marshall

Accounts Rendered Weekly.

Receipt for maternity services 1938. Only women from better off families would be able to afford such services.

Conditions in the Narrow Marsh slums before their clearance. Note the bins and the clean water pipe are adjacent to the entrance to the toilets.

The brand new Maternity and Child Welfare Clinic in 1938.

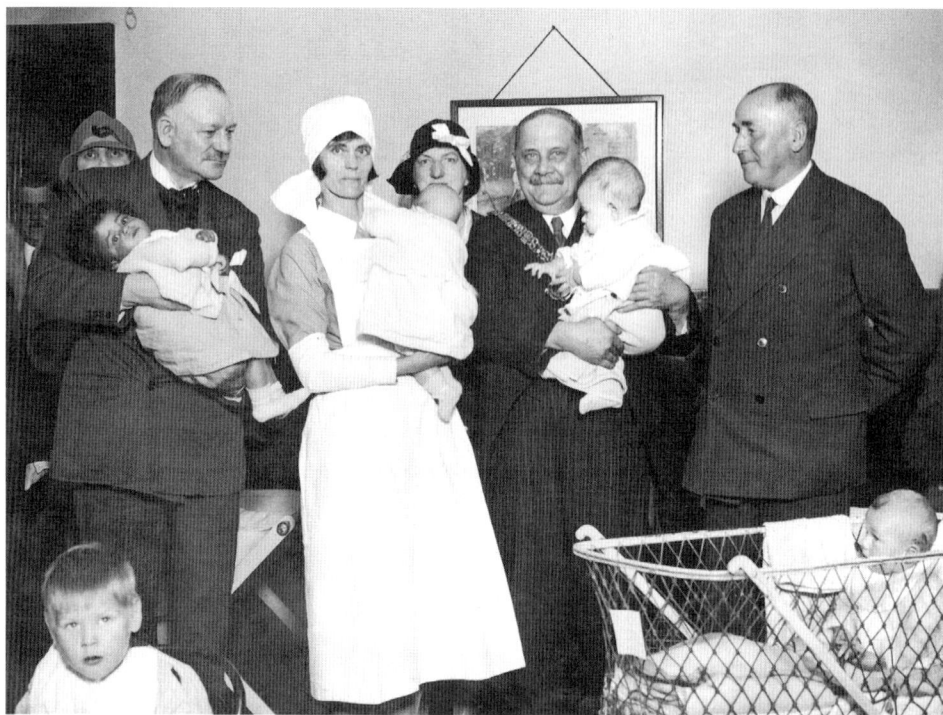

Nottingham Day Nursery, caring for children whilst their parents went out to work.

The Duchess of Portland laying the foundation stone for the Nottingham Hospital for Women in 1928.

CHAPTER FIVE

In 1908 the Goose Fair was still held in the Market Square. Two young women enjoying the Carousel ride.

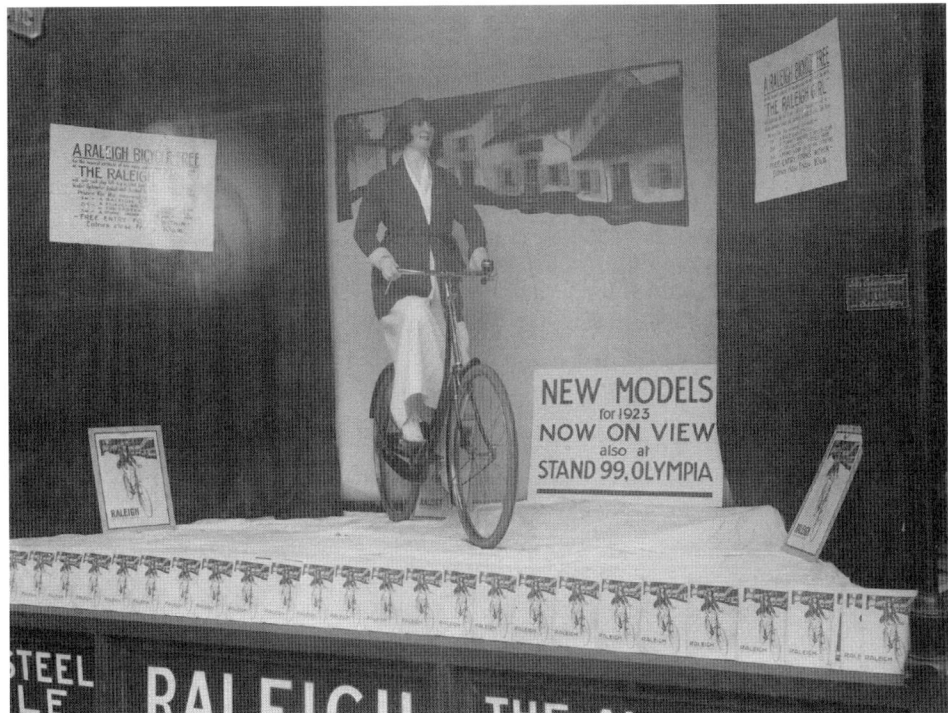

An advertising display for women's cycles, cross bar now removed, at a trade show circa 1910.

Dame Laura Knight, official artist in residence, at the Nuremberg trials 1945 / 1946.

CHAPTER SIX

Above left: *Ladies of the East Midlands NUWSS late 19th Century.*

Above right: *A postcard from a popular contemporary collection showing how women progress to being a suffragette.*

Right: *Suffragettes leaving Holloway prison in 1908 after completing their sentences.*

Left: *Helen Watts, daughter of a Lenton vicar, suffragette, hunger striker and public speaker.*

Below: *A contemporary post card poking fun at the fact that women were being force fed, an horrendous experience for those involved.*

FEEDING A SUFFRAGETTE BY FORCE.

MILK

treatment. Canon R.H. Hawkins, vicar of St Mary's Church, said that young girls had spent the whole of their adolescence in a distorted atmosphere because of the war. The usual social regulations had been put to the side while people were unsure if there would even be a tomorrow. The motto, which originated with soldiers, 'let us eat and drink, for tomorrow we may die,' was not helping either.

As the Second World War ended, the state was becoming more involved with lives of the general population. It was claimed at the 1947 annual meeting that schools were being taken over by the state and Sunday was becoming more secular. There was a much greater demand for probation hostels than for homes for girls. On the advice of the Home Office, Southwell House would became a probation hostel for girls aged 15–18 years.

The 1949 annual meeting gave an insight into life at Southwell House. The girls would go out to work in the city during the day and in the evening attended classes such as dressmaking, health and beauty, cooking and dancing.

Even after two world wars, where women had proved themselves over and over again, education and opportunities for women were based around traditionally female activities.

The 65th annual meeting, held in June 1951 confirmed that the homes were always full. In total, 2,690 nights had been spent in the shelter by girls and young women the previous year; ninety-six mothers and babies had been helped, with nine babies being adopted. Dr Elspeth Warwick addressed the meeting from the Maternity and Child Welfare department at Nottingham Corporation. She questioned the advisability of the adoption of illegitimate babies or the consideration of adoption during pregnancy. She reflected that no single girl had any conception of what her baby may come to mean to her, or what adoption may mean to the child. Dr Warwick claimed that a new mother would find that her maternal instincts would be asserted within a few weeks if she kept the baby with her. It also showed, she said, acceptance of responsibility towards the child and she would then be much more likely to accept responsibility for herself. Women of the time may have argued they had no such choice.

National Health Service

The National Health Service Act 1946 brought many changes to the healthcare of Nottingham and the country as a whole. The city council was tasked with the organisation of the new system and adhering to the new legislation. The Health Committee had to submit its proposals to the government under schemes covering maternity and child welfare; midwifery; health visitors; home nursing; prevention of illness, care and aftercare (including mental illness or defectiveness, as it was termed at the time) and domestic help (primarily for pregnant and nursing women), under sections 22–29 of the Act. The services then being provided by the Nursing Association, and many different local charities, all came under review to ascertain what was available and what was needed under the Act,[4] and ensure it was in place for July 1948, the appointed date under the Act for the regulations to come into force.

Local authorities were empowered to make arrangements with local voluntary organisations to provide the services. Agreements needed to be made to transfer premises and staff from voluntary organisations to provide the services. Local authorities were obliged to consult with the Medical Officer for Health, Cyril Banks, and also local hospitals and medical services providers.

It was thought that voluntary contributions to local charities would fall once the National Health Service came into being, as the services they provided would be part of the services the NHS would provide instead.

Family Planning

One of the issues which kept families in poverty was, perhaps belatedly, identified as a lack of family planning.

Mrs How Martyn, a key advocate and author of *Birth Control Movement*, printed in 1929 and charting the progress allowing women to receive contraceptive advice, addressed the National Council of Women meeting in March 1930. The call for women to be allowed to control how many times they would conceive began in 1798 when Reverend Thomas Malthus published an 'Essay on the Principle of Population'. He advocated late marriage as a way of reducing the number of births. The reformer Francis Place (1771–1854) advocated precautionary means.

The trial of Charles Bradlaugh and Annie Besant in 1877, in which they were accused of distributing indecent material in the form of books and pamphlets on birth control, refuelled the call for birth control for all. In 1887, Dr H.A. Allbutt had published the *Wife's Handbook*, which included information on birth control. Dr Allbutt was struck off by the General Medical Council for breach of professional conduct.

In 1915, Margaret Sanger, a leading birth-control advocate from America came to England to exchange views with those in the movement in England. Shortly afterwards, in 1918, Dr Marie Stopes published her book *Married Love*. This was followed by a Mothers' Clinic in 1921 where advice and information could be obtained. Support for these clinics swelled until the government were forced to consider the issue.

From 1930, birth control information could be given to those married women who desired it. Advice was to be given by medical experts at their usual clinics. A resolution was passed to urge MPs to lobby Parliament for the introduction of specialist birth control clinics. The clinic in Nottingham was opened in Goldsmith Street in March 1930, where advice was available to married women.

Contraception was not a subject readily discussed in women's lives, even towards the end of the 1950s. When contraceptives started to become available in around 1885 it was from back-street chemists, with scientifically untested products. One method, developed by an English pharmacist Walter Rendell, involved a vaginal suppository using cocoa butter and quinine sulphate. Spermicidal jellies were developed in 1906, although these and other methods were not tested until the 1930s. The diaphragm for women was invented in 1882 and was made of vulcanised rubber.

Given the lack of availability of these contraceptives, as not all chemists would stock them, some women had to resort to desperate measures and carry out their own abortions. One woman, in the anonymous oral history project carried out in the 1980s in Nottingham, described how she had found herself pregnant yet again. She and her husband already had four children and she was desperate not to have another child that they could not afford. This woman carried out an abortion in her bedroom with the aid of two teaspoons and a bottle of gin.

Mrs Webb, a participant in the same oral history project from the 1980s, spent twenty-two weeks in the Ransom Sanitorium in the 1930s being treated for tuberculosis; after she recovered she got married. The doctor told her not to have any children for the next five years due to her stay in the sanitorium. She said, 'no one would tell you how to avoid getting pregnant.' The woman in the next bed to her was a nurse and she sent for a leaflet from Dr Marie Stopes, a campaigner for birth control and women's rights. It arrived in a brown envelope and had to be sent elsewhere as they lived with Mrs Webb's parents and did not want them to see the literature.

A health clinic in Nottingham had, according to Mrs Webb, sent their lady doctor to be trained in birth control. This doctor then set up a birth control clinic in Nottingham, but only married women could attend. The clinic was on the second floor of a building halfway up Market Street. Each patient had a card and paid what they could afford; Mrs Webb paid 3s 6d per week. One day she met a woman there who had already had fifteen children and looked quite ill. Mrs Webb told how, after the Second World War, more people went to the clinic, which had moved to Broad Street. None of the local hospitals would take any leaflets about the clinic.

Lady Denman, Chairman of the Executive Committee of National Birth Control Association, writing in *The Nottingham Journal* 17 December 1935, in an article entitled 'Women Criminals or Women Victims' outlined what she called a 'conspiracy and silence' over the question of birth control. Many women were seeking abortions and were having to commit illegal acts, thus being labelled as criminals when in fact they were victims of circumstance. She said that hundreds of poor women (who could not pay for doctors' advice) were driven to illegality every day. These women, who often already had many children, again found themselves pregnant. They were driven by economic circumstances to commit these illegal acts because they could not afford yet another mouth to feed. Friends who helped these women were also considered criminals. Lady Denman, first president of the National Federation of Women's Institutes, went onto say that in her experience, most doctors were in favour of birth control, having seen first-hand what having too many children had done to women and their families. However, they did not want to open clinics in their hospitals as these depended on funding from their peers and they feared that funding would be withheld if they strayed into such controversial arenas. This, and lack of state support, meant that women had to resort to seeking abortions performed both by doctors and also local women in the back streets instead of receiving professional and careful help within a doctor's clinic. She concluded 'as a nation we pride ourselves on our control of public health, cleanliness, sanitation, disease, and childbirth. Why do we not make an adequate provision for a healthy race in future?'

The Nottingham Journal, on 8 June 1939, carried a report entitled 'Help Women Victims, say abortion committee.' The report was described as a 'minority report' and came from the government's Interdepartmental Committee on Abortion. Mrs Dorothy Williams Thurtle, one of the five women appointed to the committee, presenting the report, asserted that the law should be amended to make abortion lawful for women who had been raped, when it was likely a hereditary disease was carried and, perhaps most controversially, if a woman had already carried four pregnancies. The committee wanted the law making clear, especially if the abortion was to save a life or a woman's health. The committee also proposed that councils up and down the country provided free contraceptive advice to married women who wanted it, which would naturally lessen the abortion problem.

Health and Maternity

The Maternity and Child Welfare Committee, a subcommittee of the Health Committee, advised in July 1944 that three nurses were being sent to Birmingham to train as public health visitors. They would be paid £135 per year during their training and once qualified their pay would rise to £270 per year. The nurses that year were E.L. Elmes, J.E. Robertson and S.C. Hodson.

Once these women were qualified, they brought new issues for the Health Committee to deal with. Miss I. Quayle, a midwife, had resigned from her post but had not vacated the house provided by the local authority. She had not worked due to illness for five to six months and a Mrs Russell had come to live with her, without consent from the Health Department. Mrs Russell and Miss Quayle argued frequently making the atmosphere in the shared house uncomfortable for the other residents, who were also midwives. What the City Health Officer found indefensible was the fact that Mrs Russell accompanied Miss Quayle on some of her visits and often helped her with her midwifery cases. When Miss Quayle was informed that Mrs Russell could no longer live in the house, Miss Quayle resigned.

Two of the other midwives living in the house told of how they had come downstairs, having heard a commotion, to find Miss Quayle on the floor with Mrs Russell's hands around her neck. They also told how Mrs Russell had come home in the afternoon smelling of alcohol. Although the Health Officer had no objection to the ladies having a friend to live with them, to keep loneliness at bay, those friends had to be of the 'right sort'. Mrs Russell was definitely considered to be not the right sort. In addition to the alcohol and temper issues displayed, Mrs Russell was said to have two illegitimate children.

Mrs Russell, however, did not go quietly. She engaged local solicitors German and Soar who wrote to the council demanding a withdrawal of the allegations and a suitable apology. The council declined to get involved.

During the Second World War, there had been an acute shortage of midwives. Local authorities were allowed a grant to aid in the training of pupil midwives who completed their training. For the three midwives to 31 March 1944 the council were granted £551 11s 6d. Those midwives who passed the Central Midwives Board examination in August 1944 were Mary Hickey, Margaret O'Neill, Janet Esther Robinson and Annie Sansom.

In November 1944, the City Hospital should have had twenty-two midwives to cope with the number of patients, but had only fourteen. More needed to be done by the hospitals themselves, claimed the local authority.

Further staffing problems arose in the Sycamore Road Day Nursery in 1943. Mrs K. Ellis was dismissed after taking a lot of time off. Her husband, a doctor, had returned from abroad after four years and was unwell. Mrs Ellis was supposed to attend a course on 5 October but failed to turn up. She was dismissed on 23 October 1943, having been employed only on 12 May that year. The chairman of the Health Committee bemoaned the state of the profession. He said these women wanted every 'penny and privilege they could get and showed little loyalty.' He went on, saying that 'these women have to be watched as they were against, rather than for, the corporation. This particular woman was discourteous and it was suspected that she faked an inventory in August 1943.' This latter accusation was never investigated nor proven.

A circular was issued form the Ministry of Health at Whitehall on 22 March 1944 relating to the care of premature infants. It was felt important for the mother and child to have a separate bedroom from the other mothers in hospital and sole access to a milk kitchen and laundry services. The ideal ratio was one nurse to 1½ infants, although it was recognised this was impractical under wartime conditions.

When the babies were ready to go home from hospital, adequate equipment should be provided in the home, including draught-proof cots, warm clothing, hot-water bottles, a special feeding bottle and a thermometer. Women should also have access to the services of paediatrician and a home help.

In February 1946 there were two hostels for mothers, at numbers 1 and 95 Queens Drive. In February 1945, Dr Harness, a female doctor, submitted a report to the town clerk, for the Maternity and Child Welfare Committee, regarding a dental scheme for expectant and nursing mothers with children under the age of 5 years.

Rooms could be set up for the sum of £650 plus a dentist and his nurse, and such rooms were available at 75 Radford Boulevard. It is not recorded whether this scheme was set up or not. It was followed closely by the 1946 National Health Service Act and probably would have been engulfed therein.

As preparations for the burdens of the Act were well underway, the Royal College of Obstetricians and Gynaecologists wrote to the town clerk asking him to help with gathering information. They wanted information on pregnant women who gave birth between 3 March and 9 March 1946, in order to make informed suggestions as to how it would be possible to help mothers with the social and economic problems they faced in raising children.

The survey covered the mother's age, total number of children she had, baby's weight, and whether mother was breast- or bottle-feeding. It also covered practical aspects such as how much help the mother had received since the baby was born, would the mother be willing to send the child to day nursery if one were available? Had she received extra nourishment during the pregnancy in the form of extra milk, orange juice or vitamin tablets? The survey also gathered information as to the mother's living conditions, including the number of bedrooms and living rooms and the number of other occupants. The occupation of the father was considered a relevant piece of information for the survey, as was who looked after the father while the mother was giving birth!

Nurseries

One of the first day nurseries to be established was at 2 High Pavement in June 1875 by Catherine Bayley of Lenton Abbey, whose father had been a leather manufacturer, colliery owner and one of the founders of the Nottingham Co-op. By 1877, it had expanded to include an orphanage. In 1881, it moved to Heathcote Street where it was easily accessible for those mothers who had to go out to work.

In June 1878, Certified School status was bestowed on the nursery meaning that they could receive payment from the local Board of Guardians for some pauper children who were boarded out in the school. This was a departure for the local Board as the workhouse had been their focus up to that point.

At the AGM in 1880 there were twenty children on the Day Nursery Register, between the ages of 2 months and 6 years and twenty-six children in the orphanage aged between 6 and 12 years. The orphanage was moved to Beeston in August 1880 and the children were divided between two cottages to provide a more homely, less institutional atmosphere. Catherine Bayley even paid some of the fees for the children herself. More cottages followed in 1886, with donations of clothes and teaching for the children helping to sustain the yearly costs in running the orphanage.

The orphanage celebrated its 21st anniversary in 1899 with a continued need for places for children where one or both of their parents had died. Funds came from the Board of Guardians, donations from local businessmen and private fundraising events. However, the homes also suffered their share of hardships. In April 1905, a severe case of ringworm was found in the boys' home and in July of that year the children suffered from a bout of diphtheria.

The day nursery continued to be necessary as more women had to go out to work, but the orphanage finally closed in 1947 due to decreased subscriptions, increased wages and the National Health Service Act.

Pre-NHS

Prior to the introduction of the NHS any visit to a doctor had to be paid for. Some patients could not afford to pay the full fee at once and doctors accepted weekly payment terms. Other patients used schemes where money could be paid in each week and then drawn out to cover medical bills as and when necessary.

Mrs Ball[5], born in 1895, explained that her mother became ill at work and had to be brought home. She had kidney disease and was nursed at home until she died aged 40. Her father paid the medical bill in instalments for quite a few years afterwards.

The women of the National Union for Women Workers Nottingham Branch[6] worked for women's issues in all sorts of areas.

In April 1913, they were worried about tuberculosis and proposed that a care committee be formed. Dr Boobbyer, Nottingham's Medical Officer for Health at the time, welcomed the offer from the ladies.

In June 1940, Dr Mann spoke at the National Council of Women's Nottingham meeting about her concerns regarding venereal diseases. She confirmed that the best way to tackle such diseases was to educate young women in social hygiene. Munitions workers should be included in this, she said. The reason for adding this particular group is not clear, but it may be that these higher-paid women had more freedom and therefore more opportunity to come into contact with members of the opposite sex. Dr Collis added that education in reproduction, social and religious matters was also needed and that positive education confirming the danger of casual affairs was also very important.

Unfair Health Legislation

The Contagious Diseases Acts of 1864 onwards, were designed to tackle the spread of venereal diseases in ports and garrison towns. The legislation allowed police officers to arrest women suspected of being prostitutes. The women were then forced to undergo examinations for venereal disease. If declared to be infected, the woman would be confined in what was known as a lock hospital, essentially a prison, until she recovered or her sentence finished. The sentence was originally a period of up to three months. However, this was extended by the 1869 Act.

The original Act only applied to naval ports and garrison towns, but by 1869 this had been extended to cover eighteen other districts. However, no provision was made for the examination of the men who used prostitutes, and this only served to highlight the inequality suffered by women, which became one of the many points of contention in a campaign to repeal the Acts. The campaign was led nationally by Josephine Butler but Nottingham women, including Alice Dowson, joined the campaign until the Acts were finally repealed in 1886. Alice had been one of the speakers at the

November 1881 meeting held in Nottingham calling for women's suffrage. Alice was a campaigner for women's rights and raised several petitions among prominent Nottingham women calling for the abolition of these Contagious Diseases Acts.

Mental Health

The early part of the twentieth century saw an ongoing debate on the issue of mental health patients, labelled 'feeble-minded', 'imbecile', 'lunatic' or 'idiot from birth' at the time. The term feeble-minded was defined as 'persons who may be capable of earning a living but incapable from mental defect … to compete with their normal fellows.'

A large number of men had been rejected from serving in the Boer War due to physical and mental fitness worries and it was feared that Britain was breeding a nation of degenerates. As it was thought that being poor, vagrant, drunk, immoral or unemployed was associated with mental health, campaigns began to try to improve the lives of the lower class, arguably not for the lower classes themselves but rather to preserve the safety of the middle and upper classes.

The Royal Commission on the Care and Control of the Feeble Minded was set up in 1904 to tackle this huge issue. It was feared that those who were handicapped in the struggle to exist would drift into the workhouse, prison or the criminal lunatic asylums. The Commission's findings were published in 1908 and national legislation passed in 1913. In the meantime, local voices continued to call for action.

Of particular concern were feeble-minded women, giving birth to children in the workhouse. Dr Powell, Medical Officer for the Nottingham City Asylum gave evidence to the Commission. His main concern was the effect of alcoholism on both the mother and the child, during the pregnancy and during breast feeding.

The City of Nottingham had actually been providing specialised education since 1893 with the first class at Bath Street Board School. However, it was not until 1914 that schools were obliged to provide education for feeble-minded children, although sex education would not have formed part of their schooling.

In 1902, the city's School Board set up an After-Care Committee for Defective Children designed to ease the transition of pupils from special schools and classes into the workforce. The committee worked with the Nottingham Poor Law Guardians, and women from various parts of the city acted as visitors. It was thought at the time that those with mental health issues should be separated from the general population.

The 1913 Act provided for a division of those with mental health defects and the introduction of colonies for them to live in. Very few such colonies were implemented in the first ten years and opponents to the Act were concerned about the loss of liberty. Nottingham's early response was to form a Mental Deficiency Committee. There were 230 inmates in 'imbecile' wards in Nottingham in 1911. Under the legislation two women had to be appointed onto the committee, they were Caroline Harper and Mary Corner, both seasoned committee members.

The Mental Deficiency Committee was charged with trying to locate all of the people in the city deemed to be mentally deficient. The chairman was furniture store owner John Spalding, of Griffin and Spalding, although it is not clear that he had any qualification in this area that would support his chairmanship of such a committee. Lord Bentinck advised that there were at least 1,200 mentally deficient persons in Nottingham and the Poor Law Board, City Asylum and the Education Committee were all consulted. An Inquiry Officer was appointed, namely one Percy Smith; he was not especially busy during the Great War and was seconded to the local Tax Office due to lack of work.

The war meant that there was little funding for setting up services or schemes and most children leaving school with these issues stayed at home with their parents. Dr Powell was not keen on permanent care homes and when a mother objected to her 7-year-old son being sent to a home in Derbyshire, he was allowed to stay at home with her. Dr Powell also blocked a 9-year-old girl being sent to Bristol to live in a permanent home. Around eighty per cent of the feeble-minded children who were notified to the committee stayed at home with their parents.

In the post-war years, the city sent more children to permanent homes and, as they had to cover the cost of this, considered building their own permanent home. Aston Hall was opened in 1926 with beds for eighty-five girls and women. Those still in the community were the responsibility of the After-Care Committee, renamed the Nottingham Voluntary Association for Mental Welfare.

In 1933, the City Corporation finally took responsibility for those with mental health issues and established a school at Colwick. This reluctance to provide permanent care was not unique to Nottingham and lack of funding was cited as the reason. Local Medical Officers of Health frequently refused to accept responsibility for the feeble-minded as their care was very costly to the local authority.

The Workhouse

In the 1860s and 1870s it became clear that only a minority of those living in a workhouse were fit and able to work[7] and that most of the inmates were the old and infirm. Guardians began to implement sanitary and medical changes as a way of getting more people into work and off parish poor relief and these workhouses became an administrative hub for the wider work of the area, in health and sanitation.

Workhouses also accepted those classed as 'moral degenerates', which included unmarried mothers and alcoholics. While nursing staff were usually selected from among the inmates, the change of inmates to the old and infirm meant that new nursing staff had to be specially trained.

Those who couldn't afford medical treatment could use their local workhouse infirmary without being obliged to formally enter the workhouse. These infirmaries were usually just outside the workhouse and inmates were usually viewed as patients, rather than the derogatory term 'paupers' reserved for the residents of the workhouse.

By 1918, Maternity and Child Welfare Act services, which offered free pre-natal and post-natal care, were being delivered from the workhouse. Midwives became a legal requirement for the workhouse in 1915 and many mothers chose to have their babies in the workhouse from that point.

Further changes to the workhouses began in 1929 with the Local Government Act which abolished the Poor Law Guardians. Although this effectively signalled the end of the workhouse, most continued for many more years. Some unions such as Southwell, continued with little change and became public assistance institutions, following the abolition of the Poor Law itself in 1948; some of the workhouse buildings were absorbed into the NHS although Southwell continued to function in much the same way until the 1970s. Unmarried mothers continued to be looked after in the former workhouses as they were excluded from NHS maternity units, which were reserved for married women. This provision was finally taken under the wing of the NHS in 1974.

Nottingham Daily Express of 13 January 1886 reported the opening of a new hospital for women in the city. The opening speech was given by Lady John Manners at the Samaritan Hospital for Women, Sandfield House, Raleigh Street Nottingham. The influential elite of the city were present, save for a few who were away from Nottingham at the time and included the architect of the building Mr A. Marshall, together with the secretary of the building, local solicitor Mr Leman. Miss Henrietta Carey, a well-known welfare worker, was also present. The opening of a hospital particularly for women's health issues had been discussed at a meeting, in the George Hotel on 22 May 1885, with the immediate task set for the committee to open an outpatient facility. This was held on Long Row with a medical officer in attendance each day. Since that time some 1,430 patients had attended with some 7,000 visits in total. It then became clear that an inpatient hospital facility was needed. A building was located and inspected by the medical officers who indicated changes were necessary. Subscriptions and donations to that point had reached £640 with the cost of the alterations totalling £600. The works included an overhaul of the drains, a new ventilation system and the installation of a lift. The facility included wards, two operation rooms, nurses' bedrooms and accommodation for the matron.

In a speech about his experiences at the Birmingham Women's Hospital, Dr Lawson Tait said that 'throughout these islands a population of 10,000 women were always more or less suffering from only one of the numerous ailments to which women were unfortunately subjected.' Much misery was caused in very many homes by reason of the physical suffering of mothers, preventing their attending to their homes and children.

Lady Manners commented that 'if hospitals of this sort could be multiplied, the sufferings borne by women would be very greatly decreased.' The hospital provided accommodation for twelve patients, six of whom would be admitted for free, the others on payment of a guinea a week.

The Nottingham Journal of 4 March 1927, reported that two homes of rest for the poor had been erected on the Wells Road and opened on 3 March, in memory of Miss Henrietta Carey, a prominent welfare worker in the city. The site was donated by the Nottingham Corporation. The cost of the houses, some £11,042, was raised from donations. The houses were designed by Corporation Architect Mr A.E. Howitt and were officially opened by Mr W. Crane, chairman of the Corporation Housing Committee.

Some of the fine work carried out by the social and welfare organisations in Nottingham was highlighted at a conference in Nottingham on 20 March 1941. The conference was called by the Regional Commissioner, Lord Trent and attended by various government departments and representatives of a variety of voluntary organisations. The purpose of the conference was to discover any gaps in the social care provided and to avoid overlapping. It was thought that planning for the after effects of disaster should be of the utmost importance, given the recent experience of Coventry, which had been devastated by German bombs. It was recognised that there were many formidable tasks to tackle after a blitz, most of which could not be met by the local authorities alone. Such tasks as finding homes, food, and clothing, for displaced persons could be planned for in advance and carried out by voluntary organisations. The conference was a useful way of keeping everybody informed of the type and extent of welfare work being carried out.

Nottingham had commented on the White Paper for the government's National Health Service scheme and although many of the comments were positive, there were concerns that local hospitals may lose the personal touch, according to *The Nottingham Journal* on 22 March 1946.

The hospitals' survey mentioned the Nottingham Women's Hospital and advised that it become a centre for gynaecology. Mr J.H. Cooper (chairman of the hospital) commented that hospitals generally realised the need for collaboration to save on duplication of works. He went on to state that, like the General Hospital, the Women's Hospital paid its way. If the government wanted to take on hospitals who did not or could not do this, then the government should pay for it.

During the century to 1950 it was recognised that women needed better medical care and that their medical needs were unique and complex. The results were specialist hospitals, the introduction of trained midwives and, eventually, contraception. It had been a radical century and these changes were largely seen as positive. After all, women had to be fit and healthy in order to carry out their main purpose in life: looking after men and raising children.

CHAPTER FIVE

At Your Leisure

✦

Timeline of Statutes

1850 Factories Act: reduced the total number of hours which could be worked by women to 60 per week.

1867 Factory Acts (Extension) Act: women could not be employed on Sundays.

1871 Bank Holidays Act: official holidays for Easter Monday, Whit Monday (May), the first Monday in August and 26 December.

1874 Factory Act: working day limited to ten hours and the working week reduced to 56½ hours.

As living and working conditions improved, leisure activities became more widely available. Aside from the already established activities of crafts and social groups for women, they began to take up sports, something that some men found unattractive.

In the mid 1880s, neither women nor men had much time for leisure. Any leisure activities they did partake in usually revolved around local theatres and a few sports clubs, most of which were associated with local employers.

Over the course of the twentieth century, the range of available leisure activities grew and so did the participation of women. Legislation that had reduced working hours meant that, probably for the first time ever, women had a small amount of time for themselves.

Although women were making good progress in gaining rights, education and opportunities, their world was still controlled by men with staunchly traditional values.

The 'Ways of Women' section, in the *Nottingham Evening Post* on 12 February 1935 did not discuss any real women's issues. Instead there were short articles on a new jumper pattern, how to make flower jewellery and old-fashioned remedies. The adverts were for dish-washing soap, corsets, and butter from Australia, perpetuating the view that a woman's place was in the home.

The 'Ways of Women' section of 6 November 1939 still bore the same predictable fashion and homemaking advice, but was now geared towards wartime conditions. There were recipes for soups and other economical meals, together with instructions for recycling old sweaters and clothes. In this particular edition instructions for making 'heel-less operation stockings' for hospitals were given out. Young boys and girls at home were also encouraged to make the garments as part of the war effort.

A letter to the editor only a couple of years later bemoaned the lack of readily available opportunities for women. The letter implied that if such opportunities did not become available, girls and young women would find themselves in all sorts of trouble.

Sunday evenings gave friends probably their only chance to meet up outside of working hours. Groups of friends met in the Market Square, the traditional meeting place in Nottingham, and walked around the square looking in the shop windows and at the other people who were also in the square. This became known as 'parading' and was seen by some as being an undesirable courting ritual.

'Young People and the Sunday Parade' was the topic in the 'editor's letter bag' on 1 February 1937. 'Young people parade in the market square on Sunday evenings.' The anonymous writer ('No One Barred') confessed that she had taken her share of turns at this but went on to say that she did not parade because she liked it, she 'detested' it. She paraded because there was nothing else for young women to do. She commented that young women needed rooms in the city and the wherewithal to start a club where they could play dominoes, draughts and the piano. This would then stop the Sunday 'parading'. She ended by saying, 'We shall win the confidence of our young people and make them better citizens.'

Women's Institute

In 1915, and as a direct result of the Great War, the Women's Institute movement arrived in Britain from Canada. By 1918 there were approximately 800 institutes formed with activities being geared towards the war effort with allotment gardening, land clearance, jam making and nutrition.

The first two branches to be formed in Nottinghamshire were at Southwell and East Bridgford, both being formed in 1917 and still thriving today.

After the Second World War, the Women's Institute extended their interests to other areas, including protection of the countryside and footpath preservation, rural sanitation and the need for rural nurses and doctors.

The *Nottingham Post* on 29 January 1930 reported on WI meetings. Notts Federation of Women's Institutes had fifty-three branches and met at Nottingham University College, Highfields for the annual council meeting. The previous year had seen institutes formed at Thrumpton, Cropwell Bishop, Tuxford, Flintham, Gunthorpe, Annesley, and Walkeringham. It was decided to encourage institutes to study questions of health. Following lunch the women were given a guided tour of the college buildings.

The Women's Institute movement transformed itself from a productive social group for women into a powerful voice for women. Each year a resolution shortlist is drawn up encompassing issues that affect women. The Nottinghamshire Federation Resolution Short List for 2017/2018 includes positive body image; raising awareness of modern slavery; putting a stop to female genital mutilation and mental health matters.

In 1920, the National Federation passed a resolution urging the government to pass the Bastardy Bill, urging unmarried fathers to take financial responsibility for their children. Campaigns by the

Institute since then included calls for improved water supplies in villages, help for unemployed men and women, and in 1950, a resolution for hospitals to allow parents to visit their sick children.

An exhibition of the work of Women's Institutes was being staged at the Albert Hall Nottingham, reported the *Nottingham Evening Post* on 29 September 1937. The federation now boasted seventy-two institutes, after only twenty-two years in the United Kingdom. The exhibition was devoted 'entirely to produce' and included home-made jams, cakes, pickles, flowers and vegetables. The opening ceremony was performed by the Marchioness of Titchfield and was followed by cookery demonstrations together with handicraft instruction. The lord mayor paid tribute to the work of the Women's Institute and commented that one of their most 'important features was the sense of community life' brought to the rural districts.

In *The Nottingham Journal* 3 February 1943, it was reported that Nottinghamshire Women's Institutes members now numbered 3,299 according to the Nottinghamshire Federation's annual meeting. In the previous year thirty-two preservation centres were registered and four were kept open purely for canning purposes, all to aid the war effort. 'Nearly six tons of jam, 6,386 cans of fruit and 3cwt 99lbs of chutney were produced. At Laxton, where plums were in danger of going to waste, a mobile canning team dealt with 571 cans'; 134 pullovers had been sent to the Naval Comforts fund and 3,603 pies had been distributed each week to both workers and residents in rural areas. WI members were also knitting for the Prisoners of War Fund, sixty pullovers were produced in one month alone. Some branches also had their own National Savings Groups with one particular branch achieving the total of £1,765 during the year.

Girls' Clubs

Evening Homes and Clubs were set up in Nottingham from the late nineteenth century and into the early twentieth century to provide rooms where working girls could spend their evenings. It was thought that such activities would distract women from getting themselves into mischief. The events held were social or instructional and included sewing, singing, cooking and other 'female' occupations. Summer events would involve picnics, outings to places of interest and swimming.

A festival of girls' clubs was held in the Albert Hall on 17 March 1932 with clubs exhibiting their handicraft work and choral singing. Groups participating included the YWCA, Thomas Forman and Sons Girls' Club and Meridien Gymnastics Club.

Swimming

With the growth of seaside resorts in the nineteenth century, swimming became a popular pastime. Pools were being built all over the country including in Nottingham. The ladies branch of Nottingham Swimming Club was founded in 1905 and renamed Nottingham Ladies' Swimming Club in 1909. The Duchess of Portland, of Welbeck Abbey in the north of the county, consented to act as president of the club.

Matters on the agenda for the first meeting of the club, with Mrs B.J. Bloor as chair, were the style, shape and price of swimming costumes and the annual swimming gala. The gala included a swimming exhibition, clothes races, handicap races and lifesaving races. Entries came from clubs all over the Midlands.

The 1918 gala raised £22 16s 9d[1] for the Home for Paralysed Soldiers at Ellerslie House (near the Forest Recreation Ground) and a further £5 for Christmas Comforts Fund for the troops overseas.

The club held a Big Swim in the summer of 1928, later recalled by Mrs Gwyneth Cragg who took part, aged 13. She remembered vividly the 'slap up' tea in the Mikado Café afterwards. All participants were awarded silver medals.

Cycling

Women were involved in cycling in large numbers from the late nineteenth century, even though prevailing fashions made it technically challenging. It was also considered unladylike, by some. Manufacturers, recognising women as valuable customers, soon began to find ways of adapting the cycles to accommodate women's attire. The crucial difference between men and women's cycles was the removal of the crossbar, allowing women to mount and dismount with much greater ease and elegance.

By the late nineteenth century, the safety bicycle was in existence. Its pneumatic tyres provided a measure of comfort not previously experienced and improvements to brakes and saddles had greatly improved the cycling experience. By the 1890s, Raleigh was producing a large number of cycles and models adapted for ladies.

Raleigh archive material includes that of Rudge-Whitworth (which Raleigh bought in 1943) and marketing literature from Rudge-Whitworth in 1896 says:

> The Perfect Mount is a great favourite with ladies. It is specially designed to allow the skirt to fall gracefully and to render very easy the act of mounting and dismounting. It is a particularly easy machine to control. The weight is low as is consistent with the absolute security necessary in a lady's bicycle and all the fittings are of the first quality and most graceful design. The dress guards over the chain and rear wheel are neat and light and afford a perfect protection against soiling or catching the dress of the rider.

As women's social and financial independence grew they established their own cycle clubs, organising road events, races and cycle tours. Some women were even engaged as professional cyclists by cycle manufacturers. One Billie Dovey cycled 29,432 miles around the UK in one year, backed by Rudge-Whitworth, and visited their cycle shops in the towns she cycled to. In 1938, she arrived at the Pratt and Gelsthorpe cycle shop in Newark, to meet with the owners and further publicise her tour.

Literature and the Arts

Dame Laura Knight DBE RA RWS, was a distinguished local artist who trained at the Nottingham School of Art and went on to achieve national and international status in the arts world. She was the first woman to be appointed as a Royal Academician and was commissioned as an official war artist in both the Great War and the Second World War. In 1946, at the age of 69, Dame Laura was commissioned to cover the Nuremburg Trials. One of her most well-known paintings is 'Take Off', depicting airmen readying themselves for their mission.

The Nottingham Journal of 8 March 1936 carried a report on Dame Laura Knight who had recently been elected to the Royal Academy, the first woman for some 168 years. In her recently republished autobiography *Oil Paint and Grease Paint*, she tells of how she lived on a diet of porridge while at art school (1890–95), where she met her husband Harold Knight, also an artist, whom she married in 1903. She reveals how, during her early years of training, women were not allowed to draw live nudes but had to copy statuary instead.

Dame Laura continued to paint and exhibit up until her death aged 92, having exhibited her works at the Royal Academy almost every year from 1903 to 1970, some 284 works in total. She also exhibited at the Royal Watercolour Society showing over 190 works over forty years.

Dame Laura's work covered a wide variety of subjects including, landscapes, portraits, ballet, theatre, circus, animals, seascapes, race horses and, of course, war commissions. Perhaps less well known are her designs for theatre costumes for Stratford and London productions and her glassware designs for Clarice Cliff.

She died at Langford Place, in London, on 7 July 1970, just a few days before an exhibition of her art was due to be held in Nottingham castle on 11 July, as part of the Nottingham Festival.

Social Lunches

The inaugural meeting of the Conservative Women's Luncheon Club, in order to organise forthcoming lunches, was held 25 November 1948. Although this was a social group, like many other social groups in the town, it tackled pretty much anything concerning women's issues. The minutes for the first meeting[2] described the function of the club: 'to further conservative principles and promote interest in questions of national and social importance.' The annual subscription was initially set at 20*s* and Mrs Dudley Forman became the first president of the club.

The first lunch meeting was held in the small dining room of the Constitutional Club on Market Street on Thursday, 2 December at 11 a.m. The speaker was Mrs S.A. Ward, a prospective Conservative candidate in Lichfield. Her chosen topic was 'The Cost of Living', which was still a major concern only a few years after the end of the war.

The club aimed to have as many business women as possible become members. It would provide an opportunity for women to mix and discuss politics. To this end Tom Gardner, prospective Parliamentary candidate for Nottingham North West, was the speaker in February 1949. The list of members had to be closed that month at 145 owing to the limit of the luncheon accommodation.

The National Council for Women[3] offered a Chair of Music to the new university college being built at Highfields, to be funded by the NCW Nottingham and Nottinghamshire Branch. Sir Jesse Boot had recently donated ninety acres of playing fields and a hundred acres of public parkland, plus an additional fifteen acres for a sports pavilion. The university college became a fully fledged university in 1948. Fundraising events were held across the summer of 1928 to help fund the building works and the endowment stood at £134,000 by November 1928. The lord mayor claimed that endeavours were being made to meet the needs of women for higher education.

A less expensive hobby, such as writing, was not considered an occupation for women, and the 'sparkling first novel' of Mrs A.H. Whipple (Dorothy) from Nottingham was rather patronisingly reviewed in *The Nottingham Journal* of 7 July 1927. The reviewer complained that the themes of the book, and the satire on suburban society, hit a little too close to home and that the author had been a little rough on society, particularly on doctors who were responsible for the health and wellbeing of great towns. The reviewer did praise Whipple for the 'cleverness, insight and sparkle' of her novel. He predicted great success for her.

Mrs Dorothy Whipple attended the Mechanics Cinema for the premier of the film of *They Knew Mr Knight*, in the provinces. She was reported, in *The Nottingham Journal* of 13 November 1945, to be delighted with the way her story was handled and pleased that the filmmakers had kept the local settings for the film. Scenes for the production were filmed at Ebers Road (where both Mrs Blake in the film and Mrs Whipple in real life, had lived); views from the top of the castle, St Mary's Church; the Old Market Square and the Council House. Although Mrs Whipple no longer lived in the city she stayed for a few days so that she could see the film a second time.

The Nottingham Post on 28 July 1920 reported the death of Miss Henrietta Carey, a well-known Nottingham social worker, at her residence on The Ropewalk, Nottingham. She was a pioneer in social reform.

> The desire to do good practically absorbed all her energies and for nearly half a century the deceased lady was actively identified with various organisations, notably the Nottingham Town and County Social Guild, which comprised different sections of social service including convalescent homes, lectures on hygiene classes in wood carving and languages. War conditions provided yet another outlet for Miss Carey's abundant energy and the extra strain thrown upon her may possibly have been one of the causes that accelerated the break-up of her health. A daughter of the late Mr Henry Carey, lace manufacturer, and a niece of Philip James Bailey, the poet, Miss Carey … was in charge of Morley Lodge in East Circus Street a residential home for educated young people who came to the city to take up employment.

Cricket

The Nottingham Post of 19 April 1929 carried an article with the headline 'Women as Cricketers', which revealed that women in Nottingham were now playing cricket. Women's cricket was thought to be quite a recent innovation, which seemed a reasonable assumption considering that the Women's Cricket Association had only been founded a little over two years earlier in October 1926. This was not so, however, as women have been playing cricket since 1811 and even some of the larger girls' schools, such as Roedean had been playing cricket for at least twenty years. Critics of women playing cricket were mostly men, who seemed to be afraid for their own sport. It was reported the most frequent remarks were along the lines of 'they will never play like men'. Miss Marjorie Pollard, England hockey player and cricket player, commented that women did not want to play like men, neither did they want to play with or against them. They just wanted to play to their own standard.

Unusual Hobbies

Just a few months later a local woman highlighted how a hobby could turn into a passion.

Mrs E. Lewis of 31 Melton Road West Bridgford was featured in the *Nottingham Evening Post* on 21 May 1937. Since retiring after years of nursing-home management, Mrs Lewis felt that she needed a hobby. She went to the Advance club, also known as the Clarendon Institute, where evening classes were offered in practical skills, with a friend and became interested in metalwork. She graduated to working with silver and spent seven months hand beating one teapot into shape; She told the *Post* reporter that she valued the tea pot at £25. Mrs Lewis had also made the matching sugar basin and cream jug. Her next project was to be a tray for them to sit on.

The *Nottingham Journal and Express* of 19 January 1920, in a section entitled: 'Through a Woman's Eyes', had a more modern view of what women wanted. This was clearly directed at women with financial means, rather than working women. It reported how women of old usually purchased a 'little place in the country' with their earnings, whereas modern women were more adventurous and were more likely to buy an aeroplane. At only £1,200 a two-seater plane was said to be the ideal purchase. The aeroplane was not seen as expensive to keep. Its petrol consumption was said to be seven gallons to the hour, eleven miles to the gallon. As a pilot a woman would hold a Royal Aero Club certificate and be qualified to do the maintenance of the aeroplane herself. The author of the piece was all for it, stating that a 'pony can eat its head off, idling in a paddock, but an aeroplane costs its owner nothing while it is silent in a hangar.'

Athletics

The Nottingham Journal of 2 July 1928, reported on the success of Nottinghamshire Women's Athletic Club in the Challenge Cup, overcoming Birchfield club from Birmingham who had held the cup for the previous two years. The event had some excellent races and keen finishes despite strong winds. Other clubs attending included one from Boots and Humber Harriers.

Not all of women's sporting achievements were hailed as a success. Some were used as a warning to ordinary women.

In *The Nottingham Journal* of 16 October 1934, an article appeared entitled 'Women Who should be Barred from Sport'. Cyril James, the author of the piece, stated that 'there was a vast volume of expert opinion and argument to show that one of the finest gifts man could give the woman of 1934 would be to bar her from first class sport.' Although women were breaking – and creating – sporting records each season, this particular man decided that these were exceptional women leading ordinary women, or 'women who are entirely unexceptional', on a mad race that was dangerous to themselves. His issue seemed to be that the supremacy of man was seriously challenged. While he acknowledged that the modern woman, compared with her grandmother, is 'fitter healthier and more capable as a human being', he claimed that such a woman was 'denying her own sex, perverting the freedom which was grudgingly wrested from a former age.'

A committee was formed, he reports, representing the British Medical Association, The Royal College of Surgeons and Physicians, the British Medical Women's Association and many teaching associations, to consider the question of women in sport. The medical men in the group felt that such levels of sport were a threat to motherhood. 'An adolescence spent in strenuous athleticism,' declared one doctor, would 'most certainly cause incalculable suffering to women later on.' Johnny Weissmuller, the world champion swimmer, claimed 'if a girl wants to lose every bit of sex-appeal, the surest way to do it is to develop into a lady athlete.' He added that past the age of 16 or 17 girls should take their exercise very gently.

James concludes the article by saying 'there are countless others who are pursuing a hopeless and dangerous quest. We should save them from themselves.'

Such comments would not be tolerated today. Women had shown – especially during the last quarter of the century to 1950 – that they were able to use their leisure time productively and that women's talents were innumerable and varied. Even so, some men still felt threatened by these women and refused to change their opinions.

CHAPTER SIX

The Fight Back

❖

Timeline of Statutes

1866 John Stuart Mill: attempted to enfranchise women and was defeated in Parliament by 194:73 votes.

1867 Amendment to Municipal Franchise Act: women were allowed to vote in local elections provided that they were ratepayers.

1892 Property Qualification: to become Poor Law Guardians was reduced to £5.

1894 Property Qualification: was abolished under the Local Government Board Order. Workhouses and foster homes were to be inspected by committees of women.

1902 Education Act: Town and County Councils became Education Authorities responsible for their local schools.

1903 Women's Social and Political Union (WSPU): was founded in Manchester.

1906 Suffragette: the term was first used by the Daily Mail and intended as derogatory term for members of the WSPU, the more militant of the two main suffrage organisations. The National Union of Women's Suffrage Societies (NUWSS) activities were more persuasive in nature.

1907 Qualification of Women Act: allowed women to be elected onto borough and county councils and even as mayor.

1909 Force Feeding: of suffragettes was introduced.

1913 Prisoners (Temporary Discharge for Ill Health) Act: known as the Cat and Mouse Act.

1916 Women's Army Auxiliary Corps.

1918 Representation of the People Act: women property owners over the age of 30 given the vote.

1918 December: first general election in which the above women could vote.

1919 Sex Disqualification (Removal) Act: enabled women to join professions for the first time.

1919: 28 November – Nancy Astor MP for Plymouth South became the first woman to take her seat in Parliament, Constance Markievicz elected as the first woman MP for Sinn Fein, declined to take her seat when she was elected in the previous year.

1928 Equal Franchise Act: all women over the age of 21 were allowed the vote.

1929 Privy Council: women became persons in their own rights by order of the privy council.

1969 Representation of the People Act: enfranchised 18 year olds.

1970 Equal Pay Act: women and men could no longer be paid at different rates for doing the same job.

1979 Britain's first woman Prime Minister: Margaret Thatcher of the Conservative Party.

One of the most important achievements for the women of this century was enfranchisement. Nottingham women took an active part in many of the campaigns for votes for women. Although the vote was achieved partially in 1918, and fully in 1928, the work of women was not finished and they kept up the political pressure for equality. Their efforts were not just for their own benefit, but to improve the lives of all; children, the sick and the poor were of particular concern.

From the 1830s, women had been allowed to dispose of their own landed property provided that their husbands consented.

Any transaction without the husband's consent was deemed to be ineffectual in law. During the 1850s and 1860s, a campaign grew in strength for the right of married women to own their own property. This culminated in the 1870 Married Women's Property Act, which enabled a woman to retain her own property and earnings after marriage. These rights were further extended in the 1882 Act. However, it was not until 1926 that women, married and single, were able to dispose of their property on the same terms as men.

The various Reform Acts of 1832, 1867 and 1884 either ignored or excluded women from political reform. The first Reform Act of 1832 deliberately excluded women by the use of the term 'male' rather than 'person', in the Act. Following the Second Reform Act in 1867 women were allowed suffrage in the borough elections. However, at this point not all men had suffrage either, as they were not householders. The Third Reform Act added approximately six million men to the voting register.

Women asserted that if they were capable of participating in local elections they were also capable of participating in national elections. Women had traditionally worked with political parties in order to help get their men elected. They had understood how campaigning worked and felt that it was illogical for them not to be able to vote.

Other Commonwealth countries, such as New Zealand for example, had already granted the vote to women. When property qualification for the male vote was lowered in 1867 and then again in 1884, wealthy women saw men less wealthy than them being able to vote, while they were still denied. Some of these women were householders and taxpayers as well as being wealthy, but were denied the vote merely because they were women. Despite being obliged to pay taxes, they had no say in how those taxes were spent.

Suffragists argued that the interests of those without the vote would be ignored as the elected representatives would only make laws that benefited those who could elect them. John Stuart Mill (MP for Westminster 1865–8) argued that 'women do not need political right in order that they may govern, but in order that they may not be misgoverned'. It was argued that once the vote was gained, women's issues would be taken seriously.

Women wanted the vote in order to improve the lives of other women. The ways they would make these improvements varied enormously. For some it was about finance, for others it was education or marriage. In the early twentieth century men's working conditions had improved, along with their pay. Men had the vote and therefore the power to do something about their own conditions. Women had not and could not.

There were many reasons put forward at the time for not granting the vote to women. In 1892, Henry Herbert Asquith, Liberal MP and prime minister from 1908 to 1916, voiced his objections to granting women the vote. He claimed that the majority of women did not want the vote, were not fit to hold the vote and that it would upset the natural order of the country. Even in 1900, sixty per cent of working men were not allowed to vote. It was against this background that women struggled.

Women were seen as less able intellectually and emotionally; they were irrational, they could not be as intelligent as men because their brains weighed less. Women had to be the bedrock of the family and giving them the vote would lead to failure of society. Further, men felt it was unnecessary for women to have the vote as their husbands/brothers/fathers would represent their interests anyway. Besides, women were incapable of forming their own opinions!

At first some women thought the vote should only be granted to single women, as married women had their husbands to protect their interests. The 1894 Local Government Act gave all women, married or single, the right to vote in local elections if they met the property qualifications. From then on it was impossible to exclude married women from the campaign for the vote.

It seems that men were frightened of losing control. If women were allowed to vote, they would seek to legislate for social reform, which would not be in the best interests of businessmen. As there were more women than men, this was seen as a real problem.

One of the problems faced by women in trying to achieve suffrage was the disagreement among the leading women campaigners as to how the campaign should proceed. Some felt it should be attached to the Liberal Party as they were quite empathetic. Others thought it should be independent of any political party. The suffrage societies that were in existence were fragmented and decentralised which made it difficult to have one common way of attaining suffrage.

Local suffrage societies united under the structure of the National Union of Women's Suffrage Societies known as the NUWSS. The groups were still fragmented until 1907 when the NUWSS became democratic and centralised with an elected central committee.

Although the NUWSS was not a political party it did have many links with the Liberal Party as many of the members of NUWSS were wives or daughters of Liberal politicians. In 1912, disillusioned with the Liberal Party, the NUWSS aligned itself with the Labour Party. At the beginning of the twentieth century the movement was united and strong. The number of branches rose from 33 in 1907 to 478 in 1914 with 52,000 members in all and annual donations of £37,000.

There was also a second major organisation agitating change. The Women's Social and Political Union was founded by Emmeline and Christabel Pankhurst. Their policies were decided by an unelected central committee giving rise to accusations of the committee being man-hating and intolerant women. Target members for WSPU were working women. Men were not allowed to join, which may have given rise to the belief that the WSPU was anti-men. However, they regularly took advice from men, in editing their newspaper *Votes for Women* for example.

These were the best known of the suffrage societies, but there were many other smaller organisations such as the Artists' Suffrage League and the Women Writers' Suffrage League. The Artists' Suffrage League was founded in 1907 to help the NUWSS with the preparations for a large public demonstration. Many of the members produced artwork to promote women's suffrage. The Women Writers' Suffrage League was formed in 1908 and used stories and plays to promote women's suffrage.

Towards Suffrage

Henrietta Carey (1845–1925) helped to establish the Nottingham Town and County Social Guild in 1875. The Guild undertook many charitable acts including blanket loans; a girl's club; a cheap dinner scheme; a residential hostel; a club for working women and a dining hall. Henrietta was also involved in the National Union for Women Workers formed in 1895 for the social, moral and religious elevation of women.[1] The first national conference for the Union was held in Nottingham in 1896 and attracted the likes of Mrs Millicent Fawcett, a major voice in the suffrage campaign.

One of the co-founders of the Social Guild was Lady Laura Ridding, wife of the Bishop of Southwell, who devoted her time to improving the lives of Nottingham's women, not least by founding Southwell House.

Anderson Brownsword (Sheriff of Nottingham) chaired suffrage meetings in the 1870s. His daughter Helena (1866–1964 and known as Nellie) was active in the suffrage movement. She was the daughter-in-law of Alice Dowson.

In 1880, a meeting of women demanding suffrage was held in the Morley Club on Shakespeare Street. Other meetings were held in drawing rooms and school rooms leading up to the Grand Demonstration on 30 November 1880 asking for support for the inclusion of enfranchisement for women in the 1884 Reform Bill. Speakers at the demonstration included Helen Taylor, Caroline Biggs, Helena Downing and Jessie Craigen.

Nottinghamshire Branch of the Women's Suffrage Society held its first annual meeting on 15 December 1881 in the Exchange Rooms in Nottingham's Market Square. The meeting reported on the first year of work by the society and was chaired by Henry Smith Cropper, former Sheriff of Nottingham. Several men were present, including Councillor J.A. Jacoby and the Town Clerk Mr S.G. Johnson. The town clerk said that 'those who were interested in that movement might congratulate themselves upon the work which had been done during the first year of this society's efforts in their district.' He added that women would bring 'intelligence and purity' to the electoral proceedings. Miss Biggs, from London, in seconding the report added that 'there had been no other movement in England which had accomplished so much with so small funds.' She added that 'as they were able to do their work at such a small cost (£24) they might be able to have some influence in carrying on the public business of the country in a more economical spirit than at present.'

Over the next few years the annual meeting was the rallying call for the movement in Nottingham. Meetings were peaceful but often interrupted by threatening and intimidating behaviour from men worried about how votes for women would affect them.

Aiding the cause in Nottingham were the significant number of Liberal councillors on the Nottingham Corporation in the early 1880s.

By 1890, there were a number of trade unions for women in Nottingham. The Female Hosiery Union was established in 1890 and had 400 members. The Female Lace Workers' followed shortly thereafter and the Female Cigar Workers' Union came into being in 1897.

The *Workman's Times* in 1890 was writing about the need to organise female labour; for example, for the decade ending 1861 there were 7,000 more women than men in the lace trade in Nottingham. In 1897, the number of women in hosiery factories formed seventy-five per cent of the total labour force in those factories. Although the first female labour unions were organised with men's help, by November 1890 the *Workman's Times* was expressing concerns that recruitment among women workers was not so good as had been expected. These women not only worked twelve-hour shifts but they also took work home with them to complete by the morning. The *Workman's Times* called this 'the slave of labour to capital'.

Women provided cheap labour because they were neither paid at the same rates as their male counterparts, nor allowed to carry out the higher paid tasks. A large female workforce enabled employers to dilute the influence of organised men. In addition, adding female labour to the workforce also kept men's wages down. Men began to resent women being in the workforce at all.

Amelia E. Barr, writing in the *Nottinghamshire Guardian* on 28 September 1895, commented that women who chose celibacy due to religious convictions have, all over the world, received honour for this, whereas those women who find themselves single are the subjects of contempt and dislike. It was stated that, generally speaking, no woman would choose to be unmarried. The writer asserted that she should not be the subject of contempt but rather sympathy, because usually women were single through circumstance, rather than choice. She claimed that some women had been 'imprudent and over stayed their market' as single women, they had missed their opportunities and were now suffering singledom. Closely connected to these victims of their own folly were those who had been cruel to someone who asked for their hand, and had never been asked since. As Barr asserted, most men liked silly women and some even like cruel women, so neither class was fatally out of the marriage stakes. She claimed it was the weak women with privately strong prejudices that were the victims of spinsterhood. Of course, these women could also be referred to as independent, forward-thinking women, free to make their own choices.

There were many groups started for the industrial concerns of women but these were fragmented and had no common aims. Some of the groups competing for membership were:

Female Lace Workers' Society of Nottingham
Nottingham Trade Union of Women Workers in the Lace Trade
Nottingham Branch of the National Federation of Women Workers
Female Cigar Workers' and
Women's Hosiery Union.

Not only were the unions fragmented, women's work was too. For instance, in the lace trade there were many outworkers with middlemen in between the women and the employer. Large numbers of women were unemployed and the employers took advantage of this by threatening lower wages, short time, or replacement by one of the many unemployed.

Women and girls employed as outworkers suffered appalling conditions, having to work long hours for very little money. Most of the employers only gave out their work via the middlemen.

The National Union of Women Workers, NUWW,[2] Nottingham Branch, discussed at its 21 December 1910 meeting how to inform the lace workers in Nottingham of the provisions of the new Trades Board Act. It was proposed that a circular be drawn up and distributed to the workers. By April 1911, 1,000 copies had been circulated. It was proposed to print 2,000 more and distribute these at the Mothers' Union meetings. Even though this was not part of a formal union organisation, the women of the city tried to look after rights of those less fortunate.

At their meeting of 8 April 1911, the committee had decided not to send official representation to women's suffrage meetings, although no reason was given. This committee also refused a request to assist in the formation of classes for women at the college. This seems quite surprising, given their willingness to protect women and inform them of their rights under the new Trades Board Act.

This particular group of local prominent women, including Mrs Handford, Mrs Crewdson, Mrs Foreman and Mrs Cattle, wrote to their local MPs, the prime minister and the Home Secretary urging them to pass the Criminal Law Amendment Bill in its original form. They also became involved in the Mental Deficiency Bill and officially deplored its delayed introduction. It was thought that this was a desperate situation which needed urgent attention.

The proposal in the January 1915 meeting of the NUWW was to have a lady stand as a candidate on the Board of Guardians at the next election. Rather than this being adopted immediately, it was referred to the committee for discussion.

It was recorded in the notes to the meeting that efforts to involve women in the local Labour movement were pathetically inadequate and that attempts had been only half-hearted. Part of the problem was the difficulty in organising women when many of them worked outside the factory. Hostility to women workers became more of a problem.

A vivid picture was drawn by the Independent Labour Party (ILP) Secretary Samuel Higginbottom, who told of wandering through the slums of Nottingham on a hot day, seeing women workers sitting at the doors of their hutches, manipulating lace heaped on the filthy pavement.

The Labour movement in Nottingham often ignored the women of the town. In June 1906, a letter from the WSPU requesting assistance was left to lie on the table of the Trades Council meeting. A 1913 letter protesting the Cat and Mouse Act was also ignored by the Trades Council. Reports of Independent Labour Party activity in Nottingham suggest a patronising attitude towards women.

This attitude did begin to change, but only slowly. In 1910, the Trades Council had collected £45 for striking female cigar-workers. In 1911, they had agreed to give assistance to the Nottingham Branch of the Women Workers' Federation in organising an open meeting after an appeal by Mrs Young and Mrs Gosling.

Some of the difficulty of accepting change with women workers was that the men were not as organised as they could be. Many of their unions did not work together and were fragmented, making progress difficult at best. Employers were in the stronger position and men were often paid very little or were put on short-time working.

As discussed previously, the Great War forced attitudes to women in the workplace to change somewhat. Many of the women who had previously worked as outworkers in the lace trade began to find work in the munitions factories. At the end of 1915 there were three times as many women as men in the munitions factories of Nottingham largely due to the pay being better, even if the hours were longer. In 1918, Boots employed 900 women making various products for the war effort including anti-fly cream, vermin powder and foot-comfort powder. When the management reduced the working week from fifty-three hours to forty-eight hours in early 1917, output increased.

By December 1918, there were 35,000 women on war work in the Nottinghamshire area. The vast majority of these had no consciousness of unions, although in a six-week period after a campaign in June 1916, 500 women had joined the General Workers' Union.

Of course, fundraising was vitally important for these groups to be able to continue their activities. In 1913, a Forest of Christmas

Trees event was held to raise funds for the suffrage work. It was held at the Mechanics Large Hall on Friday and Saturday 29 and 30 November. The event was opened by Her Highness Princess Duleep Singh and was attended by Sir John Rolleston MP supported by Sir Lancelot Rolleston KCB DSO.

The event boasted a craft fair, Father Christmas and the Christmas Fairies, £25 worth of presents and prizes and a gift for every child. Grown-ups were not left out and had the chance to win their Christmas turkey. Trees were on display from Grantham, Lincoln, Leicester and Nottingham as well as Derby, Burton, Mansfield, Hucknall and Southwell.

In 1909, the National Federation of Women Workers held a ten-day recruitment drive in Nottingham. The Trades Board Act of 1909 had established trade boards and set minimum rates for workers. In order for these rates to be achieved women needed to be recruited into unions. The NFWW supplied two organisers to Nottingham to work alongside the Lace Finishers' Branch Secretary, Miss Peters.

In the 1910 general elections the NUWSS in Nottingham staffed the polling booths, endorsing the liberal vote and collecting signatures on petitions.

The Nottingham Branch of the WSPU was established in 1906, three years after the national WSPU was formed by various members of the NUWSS who were dissatisfied with the slow progress. The WSPU were not so patient, they wanted to force change and take the vote for themselves. Their ethos was 'Deeds not Words'.

The secretary of the local branch was C.M. Burgis, a teacher from 21 Chaucer Street, Nottingham. Leonora Shaw, the wife of a Nottingham University College science teacher was one of the founder members.

In 1906, 67.7% of the total female population of Nottingham were in work. These working-class women were under-represented at this time. The WSPU saw this trend in other cities too and had paid organisers in towns up and down the country to recruit these women. In 1908, Rachel Barrett was paid £2 a week to be the Nottingham organiser.

The WSPU intended to hold a meeting at University College on 28 November 1907. It was blocked by the college as it was deemed to be a political not educational meeting. The organisers quickly relocated to the Baptist Church on Woodborough Road. Several college governors resigned over this issue and the college later reversed its decision.

Unequal treatment and disease

Women had become increasingly annoyed at the way they were treated by male politicians. The Contagious Diseases Acts of 1863 to 1869 provided that, in and around named ports and towns frequented by Britain's armed forces, any woman could be forced by police to undergo a medical examination and if found to have venereal disease, be compelled to enter a special hospital to be cured. She would then be subject to regulation by the police thereafter. If the woman resisted, by refusing further testing, she would be sent to prison.

When it was planned to extend these Acts across the country, opposition voices were heard. Women were outraged that not only were women to be treated in this manner, but men were not being tested at all. Agitation took off from this point. Josephine Butler became president of the National Association for the Abolition of State Regulation when it was founded on 5 October 1869.

Alice Dowson was introduced to agitation for the repeal by her mother.[3] In addition, Alice was involved, in 1869, in drafting of a Parliamentary Bill to protect the property of married women, the Act itself being passed in 1870. In a diary entry of 1881, Alice commented that the local press had been silent and not reported the meetings held in Nottingham protesting the Contagious Diseases Act. One meeting in Nottingham's Albert Hall on 13 January 1879 had been attended by 700–800 women. Alice was prominent in Nottingham politics and campaigning for women's rights. She had ten children and the whole family were involved in local politics and supportive of suffrage for women. In 1894, Alice was appointed to the post of Secretary of the Nottingham Branch of Women's Suffrage. Her daughter-in-law Nellie (married to Alice's eldest son Benjamin) took over her duties in August 1896 when Alice became unwell.

Objections to the Contagious Diseases Acts were many: the Acts took away women's safeguards without full and proper discussion; women's sacred legal guarantee of security was taken away and they were in the absolute power of the police; the Acts punished the victims of vice and not the perpetrators; the measures were cruel and brutal for women and the disease had never been shown to be removed by the measures taken under these Acts.

In 1870 alone, 817 petitions were presented to Parliament in favour of repeal of these Acts. 460,000 people in total had signed these petitions, two of which were from Nottingham. A further petition from Nottingham followed in 1871, all three being presented by Sir Charles Seely, the city's Liberal MP. The petition from Nottingham in April 1870 was signed by 10,034 people and called for repeal on the grounds of religion, morality, common justice, common decency and common humanity.

In 1878, Alice met with Mrs Emily Medley, the leader of the Nottingham Ladies Against Contagious Diseases Acts. In January 1879, Alice was one of the 700–800 women meeting in the Albert Hall, Nottingham to protest against these Acts. Alice noted in her diary, after another protest meeting on 15 February 1881, that there was no press coverage about their meetings. The general policy of silence prevailed.

A small victory was celebrated in April 1883 with a resolution being passed in the House of Commons disapproving of the compulsory examination of women under the Contagious Diseases Acts. The compulsory examination of women gradually ceased and, after much vigorous campaigning, the Acts were finally repealed in 1886.

Both Alice Dowson and her daughters were involved in the suffrage movement. They held meetings at home and in large halls in Nottingham to raise awareness. In addition, they held concerts, plays and luncheons to raise funds for the campaign.

National Council of Women

Following a women's conference in 1891 held in Liverpool, the Central Conference Council of Women Workers was set up 'for the purpose of collecting and diffusing information respecting work generally but especially with the reference to all that is being carried on for the social moral and religious elevation of their own sex.'

In 1895, the name was changed to the National Union of Women Workers and their annual conference was held in Nottingham that year. 1918 saw a further name change to the National Council of Women of Great Britain.

This National Council campaigned on a huge variety of women's issues at both local and national level.

A Women's Guardian meeting was held in the Nottingham Exchange Building in November 1891; 300 invitations had been issued and local dignitaries were invited. Lady Laura Ridding was in attendance as were many of the prominent women of the county. It was envisaged the women would make very good guardians as who else could so well look after the requirements of children and the sick. It was thought that if women were appointed as guardians then men could be released to get on with business. Men did not have time to tend to such duties as women did. Lady Laura Ridding was also involved in the setting up of a Warehouse Workers' Branch of the Women's League following a meeting held at Thurgarton Priory. The resolution that was passed read: 'We promise to do our utmost both personally and by talking to others to promote and encourage thoughtful care and for the wellbeing of the factory and warehouse girls in whatever way women can help to do so.'

It was noted at a meeting on 23 February 1894 that dinner hours for factory girls were difficult as they had to leave the premises and there was nowhere for them to go. It was suggested that two rooms be rented to accommodate them. One could be used as a dining room offering cheap meals and the second for girls who brought their own dinners. It was resolved to find out how far such a scheme would be liked by the girls.

At the seventh annual conference of the National Union of Women Workers in 1895 the programme included discussion about women's work in country villages; placing out of children by Guardians; the present position of women's education; amendments needed in the Criminal Law and a meeting of Poor Law Guardians. Lady Laura Ridding summed up the object of the conference by saying,

> if we are enabled to give wise and sympathetic help to other women struggling with hard circumstances, striving to solve hard questions, and desiring to better fill their special womanly duties of wife and mother, of housemistress or friend, no one will grudge a kindly God speed to our conference.

Votes for Women – the Campaigns

From 1834, women could vote in elections for Poor Law Guardians. It was some considerable time, and following an enormous struggle, before women were allowed to vote in general elections via the Representation of the People Act in 1918, where women over 30 were granted the vote, expanding to include women over 21 by the 1928 Act. Prior to this there had been petitions and marches, speeches and campaigns, some of which involved otherwise peaceful women causing criminal damage from pouring ink into post boxes, to acts as serious as arson.

The National Union of Women's Suffrage Societies (NUWSS) was formed to promote the voting rights of women through constitutional means, these were the Suffragists. Other women considered that it was sometimes necessary to act unconstitutionally, and they were named the Suffragettes by the *Daily Mail*.

The NUWSS was run on a non-political party basis. The Nottingham branch also took an active interest in the health and welfare of women, helping to fund Basford Day Nursery. In 1918 the branch liaised with the Moral and Social Hygiene Society in Nottingham and like-minded groups, arranging a rota of visitors to attend police courts to watch over and help women on remand.

A meeting at the Mechanics Institute, to encourage women to join the WSPU, was held on 2 December 1907, addressed by Christabel Pankhurst. An unruly element hijacked the meeting and let mice loose among the crowd, then sang songs to drown out the ladies' speeches. The *Nottingham Evening Post* reported, on 3 December 1907, that Miss Pankhurst stayed on her feet for seventy minutes despite the platform being stormed. She was said to have smiled at her tormentors.

On 11 December 1907, women from the WSPU tried to break up a meeting of Asquith at the Mechanics. They had bought tickets to the meeting and security measures dictated that two men of standing had to declare that the women were bona fide before their tickets were issued. The *Nottingham Evening Post* remarked, in their coverage of the event, that the elaborate precautions taken for excluding the suffragists made the term 'weaker sex' distinctly ironic.

These women did hold the support of some men in the county. In 1907, the Men's League for Women's Suffrage was active in Nottingham. The Reverend Alan Watts of Lenton Vicarage was one supporter of the votes for women campaign. His daughter Helen was also involved.

The NUWSS was still active during this time and on 11 June 1908 a meeting was held on the Forest Recreation Ground, with an estimated 3,000 people in attendance. The chairman for the meeting was C.L. Rothera, local solicitor and coroner and the resolution was that women should have the vote on the same terms given, or demanded, by men.

On 30 June 1908, the windows of Number 10 Downing Street were smashed. Shortly thereafter, on 18 July, a meeting of the WSPU was held, also on the Forest Ground. There were eight platforms and it was estimated that 20–30,000 people attended, considerably larger than the meeting of the NUWSS some two weeks earlier. The great majority were described to be attentive and friendly. A noisy gang of men opposing the speakers were prevented from further action by the crowd. The *Nottingham Daily Express* calculated the crowd to number around 15–20,000, less than the organisers on the day but still a substantial number. The reporting of such meetings was often underestimated in an attempt to minimise the popularity of the movement.

According to the diary of Alice Dowson, the NUWSS, the more peaceful organisation of the movement, also had problems. A meeting on 5 July 1909 ended in a disgraceful riot. Police had been informed of the event beforehand but had failed to attend. Nellie Dowson, secretary of the NUWSS Nottingham Branch, was so incensed that she wrote to the local press about the behaviour of the police.

However, not all women were in favour of gaining the vote. In January 1909, an anti-suffrage meeting was held in the Mechanics Hall. The meeting was addressed by Mary Angela Dickens (granddaughter of Charles Dickens) and she said that giving women the vote was irresponsible. Thankfully, hers was a minority view.

The Women's Franchise (Conciliation) Bill passed its first reading in June 1910. The reading was attended by thirty-two women from Nottingham, including Maud, Nellie, and Hilda Dowson.

The progress of the Bill then stalled because a second general election was required and there was no time to debate the Bill. The NUWSS and WSPU joined forces to protest. They travelled to the House of Commons on 18 November to confront Prime Minister Asquith. These women were met by police officers in Parliament Square and when they refused to disperse they were kicked and punched. The day became known as Black Friday; 115 women and 4 men were arrested. The cruel way the women were treated increased support for the women's movement. Four women from the Nottingham Branch of the WSPU were arrested: Lilian Hickling, Nellie Crocker, Muriel Wallis and Elsie Hall. There was no record of their fate, however, most of those arrested would be taken before the magistrate the following morning and sentenced to Holloway prison. When women did demonstrate they were ill-treated. As Home Secretary, Winston Churchill, in charge of the police force, was thought to be ultimately responsible for the violence against the women marchers. It is not known whether he ordered such action or merely condoned it. It seems clear that no steps were taken by him to prevent such further action, as this became the pattern during these marches and protestations.

Alice Dowson wrote in her diary of the event:

> It was a critical day for suffragists at Westminster. This government continues to play with them … I was furious to hear how Mr Asquith has again disappointed us with his false and empty promises and the militants made a great riot in Westminster. Quite justified, I think.[4]

Alice begins 1911 diary with a pessimistic, albeit realistic, entry:

> This year opens with a lately elected Parliament, the second in one year, the result being nearly the same as before. Mr Asquith and the Liberals remain in power but the Irish hold the balance. Suffrage I fear stands a poor chance. Nellie, Hilda and Maud are indefatigable.

The second reading of the Bill was in June 1911. This time 100 women from Nottingham travelled to the capital to join around 40,000 other women in support of the Bill.

Once more Asquith and his government betrayed the women. The Government Reform Bill of November 1911 intended to extend suffrage to all men, and suffragists were invited to attach an amendment to the Bill if they so wished. WSPU activity was stepped up. Charlotte Marsh had replaced Nellie Crocker as organiser for the area.

Nellie Crocker and Gladys Roberts from Nottingham were imprisoned in Holloway for window smashing during the violence which followed the reading of the Bill.

The WSPU became somewhat dissipated by 1912. Some key members had resigned from the organisation in disagreement with the violent tactics. Changes were also made within the NUWSS, who sought greater cooperation with other groups looking for suffrage, for example, trade unions and the Co-op Guild.

On 7 February 1913, black liquid, believed to be ink, was poured into pillar boxes in Nottingham city centre, and votes for women stickers were left on the boxes. Further attacks on post boxes led to a fire in a box on Station Street and an incendiary letter caught fire in the Queen Street sorting office but was quickly extinguished. Post boxes all over the city were targeted.

Less than two weeks later, on 19 February, the police foiled a planned attack on Bulwell Links Golf Club. But momentum was now building and with women launching a further attack on 24 February, when post boxes were doused with phosphorus.

Sir James Yoxall's (MP for Nottinghamshire West) meeting in Stanley Street School on 25 February was disrupted by the WSPU. Seven women were forcibly ejected from the building. In November 1913, Liberal member Leif Jones was heckled during a meeting in the Baptist School Room, Station Street, Carlton. The lady heckler was forcibly ejected from the meeting by men. Other women took her place and were also ejected, causing mayhem.

Several women had been attacked at a WSPU meeting on 12 March 1913 in the Circus Street Hall, which was addressed by Annie Kenney. Nottingham Watch Committee received several claims for damage. The chief constable rejected all of them saying that the halls must take responsibility for what happened in their own buildings. The halls then became reluctant to let suffrage claimers hold their meetings on their premises.

The summer of 1913 saw the biggest march to date for women's suffrage. The march was from Newcastle to London with meetings and rallies held en route, where more and more women joined the march. Members from Nottingham joined and held a banner depicting Nottingham castle. Approximately £8,000 was raised for the NUWSS.

July brought a meeting in the Market Square protesting the Cat and Mouse Act. Four platforms were set up for the women to speak. C.L. Rothera wrote to the local press condemning the Act.

Women took whatever opportunities presented themselves to further their cause. A service in St Mary's Church in the Lace Market was disrupted when several women used their own words during prayers to call for the vote. This was in response to the Archbishop of Canterbury condemning hunger strikes and condoning force feeding.

On 27 July 1909, Helen Watts was arrested for disrupting a meeting held by Sir James Yoxall. She was arrested again on 4 September in Leicester at a meeting opposed to female suffrage. Charged with disorderly conduct she was jailed for five days. At a meeting held at the Morley Café upon her release, she claimed that change would not be won by talking in drawing rooms. She stated that change must be 'fought for in the market places and meeting halls of our county.' If women did not fight for it, she asserted, no one else would.

At a meeting in Nottingham's Market Square on 6 September, Nellie Crocker, WSPU Organiser for Nottingham, argued that force feeding, which had begun in 1909, was not worthy of a civil society. The *Nottingham Evening Post* observed, shortly thereafter, that breaking windows and destruction of property was apparently acceptable in a civil society.

Tactics varied enormously, they were not just breaking windows and tying themselves to railings, which is what the suffragettes are remembered for today. From as early as 1870, women had begun to refuse to pay their taxes. Some women absented themselves from the census of 1911 stating 'no vote, no census'. Others spoiled their forms in an act of defiance. The 1911 census required much more detail than previous censuses, some of it intrusive and sensitive in the view of those having to fill it in. It was illegal to refuse to complete the form but not illegal to be absent on the appointed day, hence the reason many women may have stayed away from home on census night. Some women did not agree with this tactic as they saw the census as a way of beginning reforms – the data collected could be used to shape the future of the country.

Force feeding, first seen in 1909, became common. Women were not treated as political prisoners and working-class women were treated less favourably than their middle- or upper-class counterparts.

On 25 April 1913, the Prisoners (Temporary Discharge for Ill Health) Act became law. This became better known as the Cat and Mouse Act. Women would be freed from prison if they became too ill. Once they had recovered they would be taken back to prison to complete their sentence. This was seen as the government playing a cruel game of cat and mouse with their most vocal critics.

The whole issue of suffrage was swamped in August 1914 when Britain declared war on Germany in defence of Belgium. Women immediately postponed their campaigns and turned their efforts to winning the war as the fight against Germany was a matter of national freedom, without which a vote for women would mean nothing.

Women became munitions workers, nurses, land girls and fundraisers. Midway through the Great War, David Lloyd George became prime minister and was more or less in favour of granting the vote to women.

By the time the Great War ended, women over thirty who were property owners could vote in national elections with the Representation of the People Act coming into force in January 1918. The age restriction ensured that men were not overwhelmed by women in the vote. This was not as far as the suffrage movement wanted the government to go, but it was a good start. The first general election that women could fully participate in was held in December of 1918. It took a further ten years to obtain the vote for all women over 21.

Local Suffragettes

In 1923, the local branch adopted a new title – the Nottinghamshire Branch of the National Union of Societies for Equal Citizenship and in 1928, work began for the additional voters being added to the registers. Approximately 5,245,000 women in total were being added to the voting population, meaning that all men and women over the age of 21 were now entitled to vote. Equality of Franchise took effect on 1 May 1929 and a general election followed shortly thereafter.

A personal insight into the suffrage campaign is provided by the letters of Helen Watts, the daughter of a Lenton vicar. She was imprisoned for a month in Holloway in February 1909, following a meeting at Caxton Hall where the attendees decided to march to

Parliament with their petition. A summons issued on 24 February took her to Bow Street Police Court on 25 February at 10 a.m. Helen Watts[5] gave many speeches when she returned from her visits to London. She explained why the movement wanted the vote and why they were prepared to go to prison for it. Her speeches were well thought-out and passionate. She felt it her duty to alleviate the ignorance and misunderstanding surrounding the suffrage movement and their actions.

It had been said locally that women who went to prison for the cause were to receive £6 a week for life from the WSPU. Helen confirmed there was no truth in this at all. She said, 'people do not realise the significance of the vote – that to us it is the symbol of spiritual, mental and economic as well as political enfranchisement not of women only but of the husbands and sons and brothers of women.'

Helen went on to explain why such aggressive tactics were used. The NUWSS advocated signing petitions, holding meetings and publishing literature. The WSPU believed that no real progress could be made until women made a nuisance of themselves and even became a laughing stock, if necessary. 'It is the big nuisances who get what they want and it is the people at whom the world once mocked, who now inspire its truest prayers.'

Helen also observed that the women who were being sent to prison for demonstrating or taking part in deputations to the House of Commons were merely exercising a long-recognised constitutional method of making grievances. 'It is the special right of those who are unrepresented on the governing body.' Deputations of men were received almost every week and, because they held a vote, Prime Minister Asquith dared not refuse to see them. However, Asquith did refuse to see any deputation of women, claimed Helen, whether they were ladylike suffragists; militant suffragettes; factory workers; lady doctors; social reformers or even women of title, despite them all contributing in some way to his government, usually by paying their taxes.

Taxation was a subject that came up many times in speeches and discussions with women. They were obliged to pay their taxes but had no say in the way their money was then spent. Giving them the vote would also give them a say on taxation. On 17 September 1909, Helen returned from hunger strike in Leicester, where she had gone on 4 September to protest at a budget meeting to discuss women's taxation and involved Winston Churchill. She was determined not to stand by and let a member of the government discuss such things without at least an attempt to let him know women's views on the issue.

Fifty police were guarding the entrance to the meeting, against a deputation of seven women. Helen and her companion Miss Chappelow descended from the lorry and walked through the crowd towards the hall. The police stopped Miss Chappelow but took no notice of Helen, so she continued on towards the hall. As she tried to make her way through the stewards guarding the building she was pushed back towards the police, who tried to push her back into the crowd. She tells of how she stood her ground, offering no resistance and no words. The police shouted at her to keep quiet and stay still. The absurdity of the situation then struck her, and she began to laugh. In response, the police gripped her arms and marched her up the street. She was taken to the police court.

Helen could not see how her behaviour that afternoon could be described as disorderly, but she was convicted of that offence, and sentenced to five days' imprisonment, along with her colleagues. She tells how, on arrival at the prison, the women demanded to see the governor and told him that due to the political significance of their offence the women declined to be treated as common criminals and refused to wear prison clothes. The governor called them street brawlers and female hooligans.

Nearly all the time she was in prison, Helen dreaded being forced, by violence, to wear the uniform, and told of how the mental strain affected her more than the physical discomfort of prison.

After their first night in prison, the governor went to see the women, stating that if they continued to refuse food, force would have to be used. The following day, after a bad night, Helen smashed two windows in her cell to let in some fresh air. The governor came visiting again and threatened her with hard labour. The visiting magistrate burst into her cell and asked why she had broken the window. Helen was taken before the governor who sentenced her to one day in close confinement. She was moved to another much gloomier cell and her book, bedding and chair were removed from it.

She ended this particular speech by stating that 'though the things one fears may be real and tangible enough, if one faces them one finds that they have no real power to hurt us'. Helen also bemoaned the fact that women were paid less than men for doing the same work. She told how in Australia, where women already had the vote, the first thing that was abolished was sweated labour – work carried out by women.

Helen realised during her time in Holloway that most of the prisoners were not 'repulsive brutal women', but were helpless and hopeless women, victimised by birth, education, environment, inheritance and social and economic conditions. A woman needed a political voice in order to fill her place in the world. She said that government by aristocracy had had its day. Women and the working class were showing revulsion for the system. Working-class men could down tools, but what if women did the same? She argued it was too late to say a woman's work was in the home, there were around 5¼ million women already out at work in industry and associated practices. Britain's industry depended upon women, who were treated no better than slaves.

Helen wrote to her family, alerting them to the fact that she would not be home. Her father was a supporter of suffrage for women but equally he must have been quite worried by his daughter's imprisonment.

In the years following her imprisonment Helen was in demand as a speaker at meetings and public functions alike. In the talks she gave at these meetings she covered various women's issues: the role of women in industry; pensions and insurance rights; long hours for low wages, known as the 'sweating system'.

Direct Action

The *Nottingham Evening* Post, 8 July 1914 reported of a threat to burn Nottingham Castle by Bradford woman Eileen Casey.

Casey stayed at the Mansion Hotel on the evening of the 23 June and believed that the suspicious hotel owner, Thomas William Marsters, called the police. She was arrested on the morning of the king's visit on 24 June. The case was heard in secret to prevent the general public trying to seek admission to the court in large numbers, and to avoid a large crowd assembling outside the court, as had previously been the case when suffragists were on trial. Local militant women had been refused entry beyond the portals of the Guildhall. Eileen was charged with 'knowingly and feloniously having in her possession four packages of cheddite explosives, a fuse and a detonator for an unlawful purpose.'

She interrupted the court clerk reading out the charge and said: 'If you are going to start about explosives you might ask why sir Edward Carson is not here, and all the gun-running business in Ulster'. She continued to interrupt the prosecutor, questioning why Carson was not on trial. Upon arrest, the court heard, she said 'we shall get our rights even if we have to burn the Castle. That will be the next. You will read of far worse things than what have been done.'

The chairman pointed out that under the Explosive Substances Act of 1883, the onus was upon her to show that the explosive was in her possession innocently. She was committed for trial to the Quarter Sessions on 27 July and was denied bail. Miss Casey had been hunger striking ever since her arrest and was forcibly fed at Holloway. She was brought by train to Nottingham shortly before the hour of the trial and was conveyed back to London pending her further appearance.

In the same year, an attack on Nottingham Boat Club, whose boats were stored in the boat house on the Trent Embankment, resulted in approximately £2,000 worth of damage and incurred the wrath of the club members, who retaliated by throwing rotten fruit and vegetables at women speakers in the Market Square shortly thereafter.

A further attack occurred on 10 March 1914 with the *Nottingham Guardian* reporting that a large Dutch barn in Bulcote, belonging to Nottingham Corporation and reported to be the largest in the country, had been set alight. It was 180 x 60ft and held 94 tons of wheat, 66 tons of oats and 156 tons of hay.

Soon after 9 p.m., some of the farm employees were going to bed when they noticed a blaze of light. The flat countryside was lit up for miles. People from Burton Joyce and the other nearby villages rushed to help. There was plenty of water available and standpipes to hand, but the fire had a strong hold and could not be stopped.

Commercial Union Insurance Company paid out £500 for the barn and £1,609 for the contents. The identity of the arsonists was never uncovered although Suffragette leaflets were found scattered near the barn. However, two women in black were said to have alighted the train in nearby Burton Joyce and asked directions for Bulcote.

The leaflets referenced a speech by Mr Hobhouses (a member of the cabinet) in 1912 in which he stated that votes for women did not have the same level of support as the Reform Bill in 1832, which led to Nottingham Castle being set alight.

Suffragists took this speech as an incitement to commit violence. The significance of Hobhouses's remarks were not lost on the local authorities and they had placed a special guard on Nottingham castle. It is possible that the Corporation farm at Bulcote was the preferred alternative.

Poor Law Guardians

In 1875, the first woman Poor Law Guardian was elected,[6] and by 1900 there were approximately 1,000 guardians in Britain. These women were tasked with trying to alleviate the conditions in workhouses, where so many unemployed, sick, old or disabled people needed to be cared for.

Once women attained the vote and found themselves elected, they began to take their seats in Parliament and then to lobby for women's issues, regardless of which political party they were affiliated to.

The 1919 Sex Disqualification Removal Act

The 1919 Sex Disqualification Removal Act allowed women to take up civil service and judicial posts and opened the legal profession to women, bringing a significant number of firsts for women, for example, veterinary surgeons, pilots, delegate to the League of Nations, solicitors, barristers, jury members and even a female cabinet minister in Margaret Grace Bonfield by virtue of the November 1918 Parliament (Qualification of Women) Act. However, this was a long way from achieving equality for women and the work was far from finished.

Women in the Council

When full suffrage was granted in 1928 the number of female voters suddenly outweighed the number of men by almost 10,000 in Nottingham, with 56,666 men and 65,956 women on the electoral roll. However, women had campaigned for election to the city council as early as 1919, shortly after the limited franchise was granted, with Mrs Bridget Jean Burke-Bloor unsuccessfully standing and pronouncing the need for housing and jobs, alongside the extension of enfranchisement to all adult women to bring their rights in line with men.

Mrs Burke-Bloor was an organiser for the Nottingham Branch of the Women's Labour League and was married to a local Labour party activist. She campaigned alongside other unsuccessful early women delegates including Helena Dowson and Annie Shepherd, both in 1919. The following year, Helena Dowson was elected to the Meadows Ward, and Caroline Harper, wife of Dr Henry Harper and a keen sportswoman, having captained local women's clubs including cricket and golf, and chaired the Nottingham Ladies' Swimming Club, to the Conservative Market Ward. Critics of these women candidates had claimed that the electorate were not ready to elect women.

Helena Dowson had been leader of the Nottingham Branch of the NUWSS in 1913–14. She campaigned for improvements in housing and sanitation and for equal suffrage for women, including equal rights on civic bodies.

Both of these women took up nominations for Justice of the Peace in 1920, the first from Nottingham to do so. They were among a group of women who had been poor law guardians since being allowed this privilege in 1892. Caroline Harper became a Poor Law Guardian in 1910 and was co-opted onto Nottingham's

Care of the Mentally Defective Committee in 1913 when it became a statutory requirement for women to be included in such committees.

In 1925, Elizabeth Webber was elected as Conservative city councillor for Sherwood. She had already sat on the War Pensions Committee, with Caroline Harper, in 1916.

Annie Shepherd was the only independent woman councillor. She was married to a bank manager and lived on Highbury Vale in Bulwell. She was a poor law guardian from 1919 and a councillor from 1921–25, in the Sherwood Ward. She was said to be 'irksome' to the ruling Conservatives as she challenged them to declare any financial interests in the public housing estates being built. She also insisted that the building contracts were put out to tender.

Women Labour councillors did not fare well in the early days. In 1923, Annie Elizabeth Wallis secured the Labour nomination for Bridge Ward but she was not successful in gaining election. The first woman Labour councillor was elected in 1926. Elizabeth Hyatt, wife of a railway supervisor, had specific interests in public health and sanitation, although slum clearance and a shortage of working-class housing dominated debates. Elizabeth remained in office until 1939, having contested nine elections. She recalled that people were 'very rude and awful' on the doorstep. She commented that she was often told to go home and scrub floors and leave politics to men. Similar experiences were reported by other women candidates.

Although women were making progress, it was slow and difficult. In 1930 there were only three women councillors, a situation that was common across the country. In 2018, out of fifty-six councillors on Nottingham City Council almost half are women, not quite equal, but getting close.

Post Enfranchisement

The vote was only the beginning for women and local action was arranged by the women's groups of Nottingham whenever it was felt necessary.

Even after attaining the vote, women continued to work for what they believed in and became involved in trade union activities to further improve women's lives.

A woman named Julie was interviewed for the oral history project in the 1980s; born in 1914 she spent most of her working life in Nottingham as a domestic. While working in Radcliffe she was introduced to the Labour movement and the Co-op Comrade Circle of West Bridgford and began attending meetings at the Co-op on Trent Boulevard. Here she heard talks by members of the Labour party and the trade union movement. Julie met her husband, Frank, through the Comrade Circle and when they were married they joined the Young Communist League. Meetings were held on Slab Square (Market Square) and Julie often distributed the *Daily Worker* throughout Hucknall, where they lived.

Frank volunteered for the Spanish Civil War and left for Spain a year after they were married; he was reported missing, later confirmed as captured. This spurred Julie on to fundraise for the war; she helped in the Young Communist Party charity shop in Hucknall collecting food for the cause. During the conflict, children from the Basque region were sent to Nottingham and taken in by local people.

When Frank finally returned home from the Spanish Civil War he did not have much time to rest before he was called up to serve in the Second World War. Julie kept herself busy again by going to work at the communist bookshop at the bottom of Lower Parliament Street. She was sent to London for three weeks, for training in setting out merchandise, raising invoices and general shop work. Following the Second World War, Frank came home and began to work in the pit at Berry Hill where he became a union delegate. Julie continued to help him with his union responsibilities and took an active interest in politics for the rest of her life.

Trade Unions

Kate Albina Marshall was born in 1913 in Basford. Aged 17 she began to work in Weldon's, sock manufacturers, then moved to Ashwell's, another textile factory, when she was 18. She told how there was a trade union at Weldon's to which she paid her 'dues' although the union did not do anything at that time. While at Weldon's the workforce were put on the dole due to a lack of work. She had to sign on every day at Standard Hill. Because she was young and had not paid enough 'stamps' (National Insurance contributions), she was not able to draw any dole money. After two weeks the workforce were re-employed by the firm.

Kate began to attend union meetings. The Finishers' Union members resented paying their fees as the union was not active and did nothing to look after their interests. People were frightened to speak out. Her trade union involvement began in earnest in 1947 when she was again working at Ashwell's, as a shop steward. She found it difficult being accepted as a female shop steward, as traditionally they had all been men. She says this was no easier by the time she retired in 1970. Kate's achievements on behalf of her members included obtaining new toilets in the works.

When nylon became more popular after the war, Kate helped negotiate higher rates of pay for the women because nylon was more difficult to handle and slower to work with, meaning the women, who were on piece-rate work, would not be able to earn as much. In addition, Kate helped to get a bonus scheme implemented. In the late 1940s, Kate got onto the Trade Union Executive and gradually persuaded more women to become interested in unions and in standing up for their own rights.

Ida Hackett was interviewed in November 1991 as part of a project surrounding miners and the lives they had lived. Ida was born in Mansfield, a predominantly mining town, in December 1914. Her father was a union delegate and was out of work between 1921 and 1924 due to his union activities. Her mother had to go out to work cleaning and washing to keep the family afloat. Both of Ida's parents were founder members of the Mansfield Woodhouse Labour Party.

Ida's first job was working in the Co-op and, as soon as she could, she joined the National Union of Distributive and Allied Workers (NUDAW). She recalled that it was predominantly men and they treated her 'a bit like a china doll to begin with'. She was also a member of the Labour Youth League at the time.

When Ida married in 1939 she had to leave the Co-op as they did not, like many other businesses, employ married women. In 1942, Ida joined Barringer Wallis and Manners (now called Metal Box), who were carrying out war work making small arms and bully beef tins. Ida worked an eight-hour shift pattern (mornings, afternoons and evenings) for seven days a week. Her daughter went into the nursery and also to her mother's to be looked after.

There was already a union at the factory when Ida joined but it was not well organised and hardly any women were members. With the help of two of the male employees, Bob Airey and Ernest Fletcher, Ida persuaded the women to join the Transport and General Workers' Union. One of the incentives she used was to give every woman who joined an alarm clock so she could get to work on time.

Eventually there were nineteen shop stewards and Ida became the convenor of the shop stewards' committee. Meetings were held in the factory so that they could report back to the women quickly. She stayed there until 1945 when the factory stopped making small arms.

When Ida moved to Foister Clay (now Meridien) to work, she set about organising the women almost straight away. She had only been there a few days when she went to see the management asking for more toilets and towels. They had two clean towels a week for 300 girls at that point. She said that eventually, most of the women joined the union and that initially the men would have nothing to do with women being in the union.

In 1952, she had raised the question of prices for piece work in the factory. The management refused to increase the rates, so she said the girls would not work. Ida was sacked, and the girls decided to support her and went out on strike. The management finally agreed to the increase and the girls went back to work, but it took a little while longer for Ida to be reinstated.

Ida's union activities landed her an invitation to go to Russia. When she asked if she could have the time off her boss agreed and said she needed to take samples of their wares with her – quite a turnaround from being sacked. Ida also stood in local elections for the Communist Party.

Rationing Troubles

Rationing did not end in 1945 with the conclusion of the war, it continued until the early 1950s. In 1947, the Nottingham Branch of the British Housewives' League, as reported in the *Nottingham Evening Post* 11 October 1947, considered that cuts to the bacon ration were brought about by the lack of foresight and mismanagement of the food stocks by the government. The women felt so strongly that it was resolved to petition the king for a coalition government to be formed.

'Square Deal for Women After the War,' was the headline in *The Nottingham Journal* on 14 October 1944. Lord Woolton Minister of Reconstruction told 400 delegates at the National Council of Women conference in London that women had achieved a great deal. It was ridiculous to assume, he said, that it was 'psychologically possible for them to go back, after enduring five or six or more years of war, to where they were before they had that new, wide experience.' The conference adopted a resolution welcoming the government White Paper on social insurance. They also urged complete equality between men and women as regards contribution benefits and retirement ages. A resolution on the National Health Service White paper in the same meeting deplored that the paper concentrated almost exclusively on disease instead of on the promotion of good health and raising the health of the nation.

It was reported in *The Nottingham Journal* on 16 August 1938 that Mrs L.A. Sanderson, of 54 Main Street, Bulwell, had accepted the invitation of the St Albans War Conservative Association to become the prospective Conservative candidate for that ward at the next municipal election:

> Mrs Sanderson has assisted her husband in business on Main Street for the past twenty years and apart from active and charitable work in connection with the Main Street Methodist Chapel has distinguished herself as a vocalist and sung at many local concerts and functions. Mrs Sanderson's wide knowledge of local conditions and experience in welfare work are a valuable recommendation.

Earning the right to vote was only the beginning, for women of Nottingham continued to agitate for change and against inequality. Many improvements have been achieved by women, for women; in small steps and huge leaps alike.

In the century from 1850 to 1950 women achieved many victories: the vote, a certain amount of equality in relationships, more opportunities in the workforce and the respect of many. However, the work was not yet finished. There were many inequalities left to tackle, like equal pay, sex discrimination, family planning and abortion, domestic violence, matrimonial property, entry into the higher echelons of politics and these challenges were met head on. Results were not always quick to be seen and progress was sometimes achingly slow. However, progress there has been and will continue to be found as we stand on the shoulders of those brave women before us, some of whom risked, or gave, their lives for their beliefs, a fact that women in this country and beyond should be truly grateful for.

End Notes

Chapter Two

1. Women's history in the Nottinghamshire Archives Office 1550-1950
2. Ditto
3. Ditto
4. Oral History Project Local Studies Library Nottingham Reference A 1b
5. Oral History Project Local Studies Library Nottingham Reference A 1a
6. Beetroot for Breakfast, Tales from the Land Girls of Lincolnshire and Nottinghamshire John A Ward Tucann Books, Harold L Smith, 2010
7. Nottingham At War Official Handbook of Useful Information and Advice Nottinghamshire County Council Leisure Services.
8. Minute Book of the First Annual General Meeting of the Nottingham Branch of the Electrical Association for Women Nottinghamshire Archives DD1357/1/8/1

Chapter Three

1. Files of the Town Clerk Nottinghamshire Archives CATC 10/120/16
2. A Pioneer Life Marianne H Mason Nottinghamshire Archives DD716.51
3. National Council for Women, Nottingham and Nottinghamshire Branch Nottinghamshire Archives DD748.5
4. Nottingham Female Home Nottinghamshire Archives DD 872/30

5. Southwell House Minutes Meetings 1916–52 Nottinghamshire Archives DD1038/1/1

6. Dr Denise Amos Combating Infant Mortality in Nottingham and Leicester 1890 – 1910

Chapter Four

1. Women's history in the Nottinghamshire Archives Office 1550–1950

2. Abel Collins Alms House Nursing Committee 1910-1941 Nottinghamshire Archives DDAC 3/1.2

3. Southwell House Meeting and Minute Books Nottinghamshire Archives DD 1038 / 1/1 and Annual Reports DD1038 /6/1-2

4. Town Clerk's Office- Health Committee Nottinghamshire Archives CATS 10/120/48

5. Oral History Project Local Studies Library Nottingham Reference A 1b

6. National Union for Women Workers Nottingham Branch Minute Books Nottinghamshire Archives DD748/3

7. The Workhouse: a lasting Legacy by Katherine Onion and Samantha Ball. East Midlands History and Heritage Magazine p 23 Issue

Chapter Five

1. Women's history in the Nottinghamshire Archives Office 1550-1950

2. Nottingham Women Conservative Lunch Club minute book 25 November 1948 to December 1957 Nottinghamshire Archives DD2416/3

3. National Council for Women Nottingham Branch Minute Books Nottinghamshire Archives DD748.5

Chapter Six

1. No Surrender! Women's suffrage in Nottingham – Nottingham Women's History Group

2. National Union of Women Workers Nottingham Branch
   Minutes Book Nottinghamshire Archives DD748/3
3. What Grandmother said – Dame Alix Meynell – the Life of
   Alice Dowson based on her diaries 1844 – 1927
4. No Surrender! Women's suffrage in Nottingham – Nottingham
   Women's History Group Index;
5. Speeches and talks of Helen Watts Nottinghamshire Archives
   DD 893/4
6. Votes for Women Third Edition Paula Bartley Hodder
   Education

Bibliography

❖

Bartley, Paula, *Votes for Women*, Third Edition, Hodder Education, a Hachette UK Company, 2007

Fawcett, Millicent, *Women's Suffrage, A Short History of a Great Movement*, Amazon

Marlow, Joyce, Edited by, *Suffragettes, The Fight for Votes for Women*, Virago Press, 2000

Montgomery, Fiona A., *Women's Rights, Struggles and Feminism in Britain 1770–1970*, Manchester University Press 2006.

Nottingham Women's History Group, *No Surrender! Women's Suffrage in Nottingham*, Small Print and printed by Unwin Print, 2016

Smith, Harold L, *The British Women's Suffrage Campaign 1866–1928,* Routledge, Taylor and Francis Group, 1998

Ward, John A., *Beetroot for Breakfast, Tales from the Land Girls of Lincolnshire and Nottinghamshire*, Tucann Books, Harold L. Smith, 2010

Wyncoll, Peter, *The Nottingham Labour Movement 1880–1939* Lawrence and Wishart Limited, 1985

https://en.wikipedia.org/wiki/National_Shell_Filling_Factory,_Chilwell

www.damelauraknight.com

List of Illustrations

❖

Chapter and Number	Acknowledgment	Reference	Date	Description
One				
1.1	Courtesy of Nottingham Local Studies Library	NTGM005519	1852	Ragged School Glasshouse Street
1.2	Nottinghamshire County Council courtesy of Nottingham Local Studies Library	NTGM005791	1880	School classroom unidentified school
Two				
2.1	Brewhouse Yard Museum courtesy of Nottingham Local Studies Library	NTGM010225	1890	Lace workers - homeworkers
2.2	Nottingham Historical Film Unit courtesy of Nottingham Local Studies Library	NTGM011911	1901	Lambert Family Housemaid
2.3	Courtesy of Nottinghamshire County Archives	DD PL 7.145.1	1920s	Players Factory
2.4	Courtesy of Nottingham Local Studies Library	NTGM011055	1917	Land Army
2.5	Courtesy of Nottinghamshire County Archives	DD 2208 -3-3	1943	Air Raid Certificate
2.6	Nottingham Evening Post courtesy of Nottingham Local Studies Library	NTGM010747	1940	Lady Air Raid Wardens
2.7	Courtesy of Nottinghamshire County Archives	DD PL 7.146.7	1920s	Players Girls
2.8	Courtesy of Nottingham Local Studies Library	NTGM012016	1910	Lady Laura Ridding

Chapter and Number	Acknowledgment	Reference	Date	Description
Three				
3.1	Courtesy of Nottingham Local Studies Library	NTGM020601	1925	Children's Hospital
3.2	Courtesy of Nottinghamshire County Archives	CA.ES 8.70	1930s	Lewis Square Housing
3.3	Courtesy of Nottinghamshire County Archives	CA.ES 8-5	1920s	Beechdale Estate Aerial
Four				
4.1	Courtesy of Nottinghamshire County Archives	DD ND 35 -2	1926	Treatment Room Dispensary
4.2	Courtesy of Nottingham Local Studies Library	NTGM011081	1923	Prince of Wales visit to Nurses Home General Hospital Park Row
4.3	Nottingham Historical Film Unit courtesy of Nottingham Local Studies Library	NTGM003582	1912	Collin's Almshouses
4.4	Courtesy of Nottinghamshire County Archives	DD 1950 - 5	1940S	Maternity Receipt
4.5	Courtesy of Nottingham Local Studies Library	NTGM000962	1931	Narrow Marsh living conditions
4.6	From "Nottingham Official Handbook" published by Higson & Co, courtesy of Nottingham Local Studies Library	NTGM003967	1938	Maternity and Child Welfare Clinic
4.7	Courtesy of Nottinghamshire County Archives	DD 1516-1		Nottingham Day Nursery
4.8	Nottingham Historical Film Unit courtesy of Nottingham Local Studies Library	NTGM003765	1928	Foundation Nottingham Hospital for Women

Chapter and Number	Acknowledgment	Reference	Date	Description
Five				
5.1	Courtesy of Nottingham Local Studies Library	NTGM001499	1908	Girls at Goose Fair
5.2	Courtesy of Nottinghamshire County Archives & Raleigh UK Ltd	DD RN6 20-1-4-3	1920s	Raleigh Cycles Model
5.3	Courtesy of Nottinghamshire County Archives & Friends of Laura Knight Society	DD 790 - 232	1940s	Dame Laura Knight at Nuremberg
Six				
6.1	Courtesy of Nottinghamshire County Archives	DD 1354 – 70 -ix	Late 19C	East Midlands NUWSS
6.2	Courtesy of Mary Evans Picture Library The March of the Women Collection	10810112	1909	Suffragettes through the ages
6.3	Courtesy of Mary Evans Picture Library The March of the Women Collection	10810405	1908	Suffragettes leaving prison
6.4	Courtesy of Bath Film Office	73/1911.	1911	Helen Watts
6.5	Courtesy of Mary Evans Picture Library The March of the Women Collection	10809905	1907	Force feeding milk

Index